Schubert

Also by Richard Baker

MOZART: AN ILLUSTRATED BIOGRAPHY

Schubert

A Life in Words and Pictures

RICHARD BAKER

LITTLE, BROWN AND COMPANY

A *Little, Brown* Book

First published in Great Britain in 1997
by Little, Brown and Company

Copyright © 1997 by Richard Baker

The moral right of the author has been asserted.

PICTURE CREDITS

All pictures reproduced by kind permission
of the Lebrecht Collection, except those on
pp. 19 and 71 (Popperfoto) and p. 2 of the
second plate section (E. T. Archive).

A CIP catalogue record for this book
is available from the British Library.

ISBN: 0 316 64033 6

Typeset in Perpetua by M Rules
Printed and bound in Great Britain
by BPC Wheatons Ltd. Exeter.

Little, Brown and Company (UK)
Brettenham House
Lancaster Place
London WC2E 7EN

Contents

Prelude

Because I am known to have an interest in music, people are all too liable to ask, 'Who is your favourite composer?' Bearing in mind that I am *not* being asked, 'Who, in your opinion, is the world's *greatest* composer?' my answer, more often than not, is 'Franz Schubert'.

Certainly the 'Unfinished' symphony, the String Quintet in C major, the *Winter Journey* songs, the *Death and the Maiden* quartet, the *Wanderer Fantasy* and many of Schubert's other works do rank among the greatest musical creations known to us; but what specifically appeals to me is the touching humanity which comes through in so much of the legacy he left.

You cannot tell the story of Schubert in terms of his everyday life during the thirty-one short years he spent on this earth. His friends, his social life, his sad attempts at love, have little significance when set against his obsessional, driving need to create music – huge quantities of music, a large proportion of which was never heard, or even known to exist, in his lifetime. It was left to posterity to put the record straight about this astonishing man. He knew he was a worthy heir to Beethoven, but his true stature was recognised by very few, if any, of his contemporaries.

Fortunately, the image of the 'chubby little charmer' offered by the hugely popular 1920s musical comedy *Lilac Time* (*Blossom Time* in the USA) has long since disappeared. In its place emerges a volatile character whose changes of mood could be baffling to his friends: at one moment the convivial companion beloved by all, at another plunged in the blackest despair, a man capable both of depravity and deeply-felt remorse. His real existence was at his desk, filling reams of music paper with millions of notes, drawing inspiration from the poets whose words he transmuted into song, and finding it hard to keep pace with an almost incessant flow of musical ideas.

I am well aware that this book is one more addition to the flood of printed and recorded material which has greeted the 200th anniversary of Schubert's birth on 31 January 1797, but I can only hope that you will share my own intense pleasure at discovering more about my favourite composer. I owe a great debt of gratitude to my researcher and collaborator Rosie Cox, without whom the task would have been impossible.

Richard Baker

April 1997

. I .

Schubert's Vienna

In the late eighteenth century Vienna was without doubt the musical capital of Europe. It was in Vienna in 1781 that Mozart decided to shake himself free from the shackles that bound him to provincial Salzburg. Returning to Vienna in 1790, Haydn felt a great sense of release; his employer Prince Nicholas Esterházy had just died, thus absolving his long-serving Kapellmeister from his obligation to spend long periods in a remote Hungarian castle. Two years later, the young Beethoven came to Vienna to take lessons from Haydn, and the city henceforth became his home. There he quickly built a formidable reputation both as composer and keyboard performer, and he was able to command the allegiance of many an aristocratic patron, despite the fact that disrespect for rank was almost a religion with him.

Beethoven's determination not to doff his cap to authority has to be seen in the context of the French Revolution and its effects. The last decade of the eighteenth century and the first of the nineteenth were years of huge turmoil, and by no means only in France. The old order was threatened everywhere, and Beethoven for one welcomed the fact: to him Napoleon, as an agent of the revolution, was a hero – until he assumed dictatorial powers and threatened to become a tyrant himself.

*Central Vienna, with St
Stephen's Cathedral, twenty
years before Schubert's birth*

Central Vienna, with St Stephen's Cathedral, twenty years before Schubert's birth

When Schubert was born in January 1797, Napoleon's armies were inflicting defeat on the Austrians in the territories they held in northern Italy. Napoleon then crossed the Alps, captured Graz and seemed likely to push on to Vienna. In April an Austrian army set out to defend the capital, but rather than fight, Napoleon signed a peace treaty with Austria, though he had no intention of honouring it.

In 1805, when Schubert was eight, Napoleon's army did attack and occupy Vienna: the first performance of Beethoven's *Fidelio* had to be given before an audience of French officers. For a time the French were driven out, but in 1809, when Schubert was twelve, Vienna was once again occupied by foreign troops. They entered the city after just one day's fighting, during which French artillery made a hole in the buildings of the boy's school.

The liberal ideals which had inspired the French Revolution in the first place had all but perished in the tidal wave of military conquest which followed it, and the Austrian Emperor could rely on the patriotic resistance of most citizens of Vienna, the Schubert family among them. Some of Franz Schubert's earliest compositions were battle songs. In November 1813 he celebrated victory at the battle of

Leipzig with a canon for three male voices called 'On the Victory of the Germans', and another of his songs, 'Who is Great?', for solo bass and orchestra, set a gushing text in praise of the Emperor.

But that Emperor was no liberal. In 1792 Francis II had succeeded his father, the 'enlightened' Joseph II. Fearing revolution in his own country, Francis set up, in the years following the final defeat of Napoleon in 1815, what amounted to a police state. Backed by the powerful and reactionary Prince von Metternich, he kept watch on his subjects through a network of spies. Literature and the stage were censored, public assemblies were restricted, travel was forbidden without a permit and student associations were banned. One of Schubert's close companions, the poet and academic Johann Senn, was banished from Vienna after a police raid on his rooms in March 1820: all he had done was to protest to the authorities about their treatment of a fellow student. In 1823 Schubert attracted the attention of the police by collaborating with the dramatist Ignaz Castelli to produce a satirical light opera based on Aristophanes' *Lysistrata*: it concerned a revolt by neglected wives against their husbands' devotion to war. It was originally called *Die Verschworenen* (*The Conspirators*), and the censor thought that altogether too subversive. So the title had to be changed to *Der Häusliche Krieg* (*The Domestic War*). The piece had to wait for a performance until 1861. Nor did Schubert witness a performance of another opera of his for similar reasons: *Der Graf von Gleichen* was banned altogether in October 1826 because it referred to bigamy on the part of a nobleman.

Charles Sealsfield, author of *Austria As It Is* (1828), reported thus on the plight of Austrian writers at that time:

Napoleon I

A more fettered being than an Austrian author surely never existed . . . [He] must not offend against any government nor against any minister; nor against any hierarchy if its members be influential; nor against the aristocracy. He must not be liberal, nor philosophical, nor humorous — in short he must be nothing at all. What would have become of Shakespeare if he had been doomed to live and write in Austria?

*Congress of Vienna: the
delegates enjoyed dancing
more than debating*

His prospects would have been gloomy, for Shakespeare's plays, popular at that period in Vienna, were censored by the Emperor's agents.

Schubert did little to promote his chances of an official appointment (not that he sought one with any eagerness) through his association with politically questionable wordsmiths but, fortunately for him, music without words was exempt from the attentions of official vigilantes. This was a wise move on the part of the government for, as one commentator put it, the only thing that was likely to turn the Viennese against the Emperor was a ban on dancing and the music that went with it.

The waltz had arrived in Vienna around 1780. Thirty years later it had become an obsession. Dance-halls were springing up all over the city, and on a single night in the carnival season of 1821, it is said there were 1,600 balls going on, most of them lasting till dawn. As early as 1787, Mozart's first Don Basilio in *The Marriage of Figaro*, the Irish tenor Michael O'Kelly, wrote of 'waltzing from ten at night till seven in the morning'. He went on:

The passion for dancing . . . was so pronounced among Viennese ladies that nothing would make them curtail their favourite amusement. This went so far that for expectant mothers who could not be induced to stay at home, separate rooms were provided . . . in which the child could be brought into the world if unhappily this should prove necessary.

A passion for dancing: all Vienna was in love with the waltz

When in September 1814 European diplomats gathered in the Austrian capital to hammer out a new order for Europe in the wake of the Napoleonic upheavals, the waltz seems to have got in the way of the proceedings. As the Prince de Ligne remarked to a friend: '*Le Congrès ne marche pas, il danse.*' (The congress makes no progress, but it dances.) No doubt many of the visitors were happy enough to join the Viennese in their relentless pursuit of pleasure, pausing only for an hour or two in the carnival season from the gyrations of the dance and occupying those hours with the pleasures of the table.

Schubert helped to sustain the mania for dancing among his friends by composing, or improvising at the piano, scores of waltzes and other dances. He would not have felt at home in the vast halls of the city's major ballrooms, among them the Apollo which could accommodate 4,000 revellers each evening. His preferred ambience was more intimate, a favourite café perhaps, or the home of one of his friends.

These informal domestic gatherings were a sign of the times. No longer was private music-making confined to the palaces of the great; every middle-class family aspired to the possession of a piano (indeed, the banker Von Geymuller had one for each of his five daughters) and it wasn't unusual for families, the Schuberts among them, to form their own string quartets. 'Very often,' wrote Hans Normann five years after Schubert's death, 'one hears in a house a violin playing on the ground floor, a piano on the first floor, a flute on the second, singing and guitar on the third, while, into the bargain, in the courtyard, a blind man exerts himself on the clarinet.' A few decades earlier the English music traveller Charles Burney had gone so far as to claim that 'even the angels over the door sing'.

Musical education had a high priority, for musical accomplishment was considered a passport to a prosperous future for men as well as women. As the *Allgemeine Musikalische Zeitung* (*General Musical News*) commented in 1800: 'Many a fellow has musicked himself to the side of a rich wife or into a highly lucrative position.'

Such people provided musically literate audiences for the city's seven concert venues and five theatres, four of them dedicated to opera. They also enhanced attendances at Vienna's forty-eight churches, especially the Imperial Court Chapel and St Stephen's Cathedral, where music played a very important role in the proceedings. To the detriment of religion, some felt, for as Charles Sealsfield found in the 1820s, the Viennese often flocked to high Mass not to pray but to listen to the music. When that was over, 'the whole crowd hastens to the door, leaving priests, divine service, everything, to do its business alone'. Although Schubert composed a considerable amount of church music, he seems to have had no love of institutional religion: his famous 'Ave Maria' was not written for the church and arose, said Schubert, from spontaneous religious feeling.

Ludwig van Beethoven, c. 1814. Vienna's musical world acknowledged his genius

A change seems to have occurred in Viennese musical taste around the time of the Congress of Vienna. Until then there was widespread interest in serious new music. The première of Beethoven's First Symphony took place at a typically gargantuan musical feast in the year 1800; it also included music by Mozart and Haydn as well as the first performance of Beethoven's Septet. Another Beethoven marathon in December 1808 introduced both the Fifth and Sixth Symphonies to the Viennese public. They were at least prepared to listen, though some of those present found the Fifth disturbing. The French musician Jean-Francois Lesueur exclaimed to the young Berlioz: 'Ouf! Let me get out; I must have air. It's incredible!

Domenico Barbaja, operatic
impresario

Marvellous! It has so upset and bewildered me that when I wanted to put on my hat, I couldn't find my head!'

Vienna conferred the freedom of the city on Beethoven in 1815 and his funeral in 1827 was a national occasion, but, in between, the general Viennese public appeared to lose interest. In 1822 Beethoven told a journalist: 'You will hear nothing of me here. My music went out of fashion long ago, and here fashion is everything.'

What had become fashionable was opera, and above all the operas of Rossini. For the most part light-hearted and frothy, they offered escape just as the waltz did in the ballroom. Serious thought, which could lead to trouble with the secret police, was not called for.

The man responsible for introducing Italian opera to Vienna was Domenico Barbaja, a remarkable impresario who was among the first to recognise Rossini's genius. From a humble start as a kitchen hand in cafés, he went on to rebuild and run the San Carlo opera house in Naples and later managed La Scala in Milan. He is important in this story because from 1821–28 he ran the Theater an der Wien and the Kärntnertor Theatre in Vienna. Barbaja lost his mistress, the singer Isabella Colbran, to Rossini, who made her his wife, but managed to remain Barbaja's friend.

By the time of Rossini's first visit to Vienna in 1822, the Rossini craze had reached overwhelming proportions. The composer's reception gala was 'like an idolatrous orgy', wrote a Leipzig newspaper reporter: 'Everyone there acted as if he had been bitten by a tarantula; the shouting, crying and yelling went on and on.' Observing the scene through British eyes, Sealsfield declared that 'a new opera of Rossini in the Kärntnertor Theatre will, with these good people, produce quite as much and even more excitement than the opening of Parliament in London'.

Ludwig Rellstab, some of whose poems were set by Schubert in his *Schwanengesang*, summed up the situation thus: 'Since the Italians have taken such a hold here, the best art is in jeopardy. The nobility has no eyes for anything but ballet, no feeling for anything except race-horses and dancing girls.'

As we shall see, Schubert admired Rossini as much as anyone. 'You can't deny that he has extraordinary genius,' he wrote in a letter of May 1819, and he would dearly have liked to rival Rossini's success in the musical theatre. Perhaps Schubert's disappointment in this field was to the benefit of posterity in that Schubert was forced to follow his own highly individual path instead.

When Chopin was in Vienna in 1829 and again in 1831, he was disgusted by the superficiality of Viennese taste. When Schumann thought of settling there, he was shocked that a city which was supposed to be so in love with music should in fact be so indifferent to it. What the Viennese loved was bravura display, in the opera house or on the concert platform. Paganini's concerts of 1828 were the most popular and lucrative musical events in Viennese history. The city went Paganini-mad, to the extent that food and articles of clothing were named after him.

Gioacchino Rossini, admired and envied by Schubert

The most commercially successful type of concert (Paganini apart) would typically include an opera overture, a concerto movement played by a famous virtuoso, a set of variations on a popular tune played on some novel instrument such as the czaka or musical walking stick, with some big blockbuster to guarantee a wild ovation at the end. 'How little propensity the Viennese have for serious music was sufficiently proved when Haydn's *Creation* was performed in the Imperial Riding School by 350 musicians. Though the grandest performance I ever witnessed it was but thinly attended,' Sealsfield noted.

There were, of course, intellectuals who deplored the mania for 'empty virtuosity' and championed the cause of serious art music. A group of them got together in 1812 to form the Society of the Friends of Music (Gesellschaft der Musikfreunde). Their regular concerts featured whole symphonies and concertos, especially those of Beethoven, and in 1818 they started a series of Thursday evening concerts which were held in small venues and featured chamber music and songs, including some by Schubert. The society paid fees and was a very welcome source of income for professional musicians:

Paganini: they said he was in league with the devil

the cult of the amateur did not help those who sought to make a living from music.

Yet in a curious way it *did* help Schubert. He failed in the only two applications he made for official appointments, and only during the summers of 1818 and 1824 did he have a paid job, as music teacher to the two daughters of Count Esterházy in Hungary. He only gave one full-scale public concert in his life. That he was able to survive at all was thanks to the generosity of easy-going friends and to the growth of domestic music-making. Schubert's prolific output of works on an intimate scale made it possible for his friends to organise many musical evenings in their homes, devoted entirely, or almost entirely, to Schubert pieces; for these the special name of 'Schubertiad' was devised. There would be plenty of music, with Schubert presiding at the piano, followed by eating and drinking and party games. All this accorded with what Frances Trollope, writing in 1836, called 'the universal spirit of gaiety' which prevailed in the city at the time, fostered by the government as 'one of the surest means of keeping the minds of the people from gloomy discontent'.

The average Viennese person was probably content enough. You didn't have to be rich to enjoy the sheer beauty of the city, with country walks readily to hand and many fine public gardens and parks filled in the summer with people strolling happily around or dancing to the tune of bands playing the popular music of the day. There were frequent festivals, none more splendid than the Great Spring Festival on St Bridget's day, 1 May. Then fire-eaters, sword-swallowers, acrobats, menageries and fireworks combined with music of every kind to provide constant amusement, and there were plenty of people ready to revel in it all non-stop until the dawn of the morning after.

Most extensive of the city's open spaces was the Prater. As Frances Trollope wrote in 1836:

> In size it is so magnificent that our three parks and Kensington Gardens to boot might be placed within it . . . [There] every evening during the fine season those strains of music may be heard which seem to form as necessary a part of the existence of an Austrian as the air he breathes. This singularly strong national besoin of amusement and music . . . which is not only unchecked but cherished by the authorities, furnishes in my belief one of the principal keys to the mystery of the superior tranquillity and contentment of the populace of this country over that of any other.

How appropriate that the Mayor of Vienna from 1804–23 should be one Stefan von Wohlleben – 'Stephen of the Good Life'!

The quintessential Viennese citizen of the period from 1815–48 was defined in a series of satirical pieces which appeared between 1855–57 in the magazine *Fliegende Blätter* (*Flying Leaves*). Their creation, Gottlieb Biedermeier (literally 'God-loving honest fellow'),

Promenade in the Prater

gave his name to this whole epoch. The first half of the nineteenth century, known to the Viennese as Alt Wien (old Vienna), was subsequently labelled the 'Biedermeier' period. Biedermeier himself was domesticated, cosy, self-confident and smug, all of which qualities add up to the beloved *gemütlichkeit* of the Viennese. He cared little for politics and dismissed everything beyond his limited horizon with a shrug of the shoulders. His creators made him a schoolmaster, the profession of Schubert's law-abiding father and one the composer himself was forced to adopt for a time.

When Schubert senior came to Vienna in 1783, education was well-regarded in the city. The Empress Maria Theresa (1717–80) had given education a high priority, launching a thorough reform of the Austrian school system and changing attitudes to the teaching profession. Formerly regarded as lowly creatures, teachers were now put into official uniforms and became respected individuals. Maria

Theresa's co-ruler from 1765 and successor when she died, her son Emperor Joseph II, shared his mother's zeal for education and continued her reforms, only to have them all undone by *his* son, who became the Emperor Francis II in 1792. Francis went so far as to tell a deputation of schoolmasters: 'I don't need scholars, I need obedient subjects.' His only saving grace from the young Schubert's point of view was that he did approve of musical education.

The financial rewards of teaching were not great and the Schubert family, like others of their kind, were made poorer by the war against Napoleon, what with special taxes for the defence of Vienna, inflation and even state bankruptcy in 1811. But the Schuberts were used to making a little go a long way, and there's no evidence that they ever went hungry. Few Viennese did – the fertile agricultural land around the city saw to that. Indeed, a wartime soup kitchen set up to feed the poor had to close after twenty days for lack of customers. Recovery from the war was rapid, and by 1820 living was cheaper in Vienna than in most other large cities. Food was apparently abundant, and in 1824 the travel writer James Holman complained: 'In Vienna they do nothing but eat.'

No doubt it was another expression of the Viennese talent for turning their backs on their troubles, which in the early nineteenth century included the hazards faced by the inhabitants of any large city at the time. Infant mortality was high and life expectancy low. Men lived on average for between thirty-six and forty years; women slightly longer, between forty-one and forty-five years. So although Schubert's death at the age of thirty-one was tragically early by our reckoning, it was not so shocking by the standards of the time.

Many women died in childbirth, so second and third marriages were quite common. Schubert's father married twice and had nineteen children, only nine of whom survived: Schubert's brother Ferdinand, who also married twice, had twenty-eight children, sixteen of whom died young.

Impure drinking water and inadequate sewage-disposal presented constant dangers to health. TB, typhus and venereal disease were endemic. In 1806 there were 2,330 deaths from smallpox, and in 1831 1,953 people died of cholera. Almost incredibly the Viennese managed to make light even of these ghastly visitations, dancing while the cholera epidemic was raging to 'Cholera Gallopades'!

Schubert was thoroughly Viennese in his enjoyment of convivial entertainment, but he had an almost Mahlerian awareness of the skull beneath the skin. The clouds which cross the sky as major shifts to minor in his music are not the fluffy kind that blow away with the slightest breeze, and the darkness which could envelop his world like an eclipse sometimes left even his most sympathetic hearers baffled. When Schubert first performed his *Winter Journey* cycle to a group of intimate, admiring friends, the only song they appeared to like was the gently nostalgic 'Frühlingsträum' ('Dream of Spring'). Like their fellow citizens they preferred agreeable fantasy to hard fact. They found it hard to confront the abiding realities of the human condition, from which Schubert and the poets who inspired him had no escape.

. II .

Schubert at School

Schubert's father, Franz Theodor, came from a farming family in Moravia. In January 1785, less than two years after he moved to Vienna, he married Elizabeth Vietz, who was in domestic service and whose father had been a locksmith in Silesia. His professional reputation was dubious, but the Vietz family included musicians and artists, so there were perhaps genetic reasons why Franz Theodor and Elizabeth should have produced a musical genius.

Elizabeth was kept extremely busy bearing children. Her first, Ignaz, was born two months after her wedding, and when Franz Peter Schubert arrived on 31 January 1797, he was the twelfth of fourteen children. Only four apart from Franz survived into adulthood: his elder brothers Ignaz, Ferdinand and Karl and his sister Theresa. Their mother died of typhus at the age of fifty-six in May 1812. Thirteen months later Franz Theodor remarried, but that was not considered surprising: very few widowers in Vienna at that time remained so for more than a year.

The house where Schubert was born has been preserved as a museum. Called 'The Red Crayfish', it is situated on the Himmelpfortgrund (literally 'the ground of the heavenly gate') in the north-western part of the city. More than one family shared the

Schubert's father, the schoolmaster Franz Theodor

house, and the Schuberts' quarters had to provide both living accommodation and schoolrooms. Conditions were incredibly cramped, but under Franz Theodor the school acquired a good reputation, and when Franz was four, the family was able to move into larger premises, a house called 'The Black Horse' in the nearby Säulengasse.

Even there, space was limited. The school's 180 pupils (including, until he was eleven, Schubert) occupied two large ground-floor rooms in two shifts, half of them in the morning and half in the afternoon. Franz Theodor was obliged by law to teach poor children for nothing, and since the school was in a poor area he had barely enough fee-paying pupils to cover the cost of teaching materials and assistant teachers: their salaries had to be provided in those days by the headmaster. No wonder Franz Theodor tried to persuade his sons to become teachers: that way he could save a lot of money. He was essentially a good, conscientious father, if rather conservative in politics and religion. The radical views of his eldest son Ignaz, who supported the liberal reforms of the Emperor Joseph II, must have been anathema to him. It was Ferdinand, nine years younger than Ignaz, who was eventually to take over the role of head of the family after Franz Theodor died on July 1830, eighteen months after his composer son.

Ferdinand was destined to play an important role in Franz Peter's life, but it was brother Ignaz, his senior by twelve years, who gave him his first piano lessons at the age of seven. Already there were traces of that inner assurance which in later years was to develop into Schubert's firm belief in his own genius. 'I was astonished,' recalled Ignaz, 'when [Franz] told me he no longer needed any tuition from me and that in future he'd manage by himself. In a short space of time he made such progress that I was forced to recognise him as a master who had surpassed me and whose standard I could never hope to achieve.'

Practising the piano in the Schubert household was a problem. The family did own an instrument but it was old and worn out, and the house was full of noisy schoolchildren during the day. Nor can it have been quiet at other times. In the year that Schubert started to play, his uncle Karl died, and his parents assumed responsibility for

Karl's three children as well as their own. Fortunately, a relative was able to arrange for the talented young Schubert to continue his programme of self-instruction on a keyboard at a piano warehouse.

In fact, all the Schubert boys played the piano up to a point, and a stringed instrument too. All schoolmasters in Germany and Austria had to be competent musicians, and Franz Schubert senior, whose main instrument was the cello, started young Schubert on the violin. Later he graduated to the viola, and from about 1810 the Schubert family had their own string quartet. Ferdinand and Ignaz played violin, Franz junior the viola and Franz senior the cello. By all accounts the father was the weakest member of the ensemble, and the story goes that he would sometimes have to be gently called to order by young Schubert during their Sunday afternoon practice sessions. If Schubert senior played a wrong note, his son would give the signal to stop and say with the greatest respect: 'Father, I don't think that was quite right.'

In 1805, when Schubert was eight, his father sent him to Michael

The courtyard of the house where Schubert was born

Holzer, choirmaster of nearby Liechtenthal parish church, for singing, piano and organ lessons. He was soon leading the trebles in the choir and playing violin solos from the organ loft. Described as 'a bibulous but competent contrapuntist', Holzer was as surprised as brother Ignaz by young Schubert's musical precocity. 'If I wanted to teach him anything new,' he recalled later, 'he already knew it. So I gave him no actual tuition but merely talked to him and watched in silent astonishment.'

When Franz was eleven, an opportunity occurred which opened the way to the best education then available in Vienna, musical or otherwise. On 3 August 1808, the *Wiener Zeitung* advertised for candidates to fill vacancies in the Imperial chapel choir. They had to be 'well instructed in singing', 'fit to enter the top Latin class' and 'past the danger of smallpox'. Young Schubert survived the tests conducted by the choirmaster, Philipp Korner, and the Imperial Kapellmeister himself, Antonio Salieri, with the result that he was offered a choral scholarship which carried with it a free place at the Imperial and Royal Seminary, otherwise known as the Konvikt. The

Konvikt had a formidable academic reputation, helped no doubt by its
iron discipline. The boys were told from day one that failure in any
subject would result in dismissal. Apart from its activities as a school,
the Konvikt also served as a hall of residence for adult scholars drawn
to Vienna from other parts of the Austrian Empire.

Schubert was extraordinarily lucky because the Imperial seminary
was not subject to the general lowering of educational standards
which had taken place since the accession of the Emperor Francis.
The Emperor loved his music and derived great pleasure from playing
second violin in a string quartet, so he continued to support the choir
school with government funds and scholarships.

*Schubert's brother Ignaz:
schoolboy Franz asked him
for extra pocket money*

The Konvikt was in some ways like a musical conservatoire. Its
director, Dr Innocenz Lang, was a keen musician and saw to it that
time was allowed for solo practice, chamber music and daily rehearsals
of the school orchestra. These took place every evening, except during
the occupation of Vienna in 1809; on special occasions the orchestra
performed before an invited audience, with the windows thrown open
so that people gathered outside could listen. Sometimes chairs were
provided for the eavesdroppers, and such were the crowds that traffic
was brought to a standstill. The school orchestra was of great importance to Schubert, who quickly rose through the ranks to become
leader and deputy conductor, gaining on the way an introduction to
the symphonies of Mozart, Haydn and Beethoven, as well as the
opportunity to try out his own earliest symphonies. The regular conductor of the orchestra was Wenzel Ruzicki, court organist and viola
player at Vienna's Burgtheater. Asked by Salieri to give Schubert special lessons in counterpoint, he soon reported that he felt redundant,
for as far as he could see the boy had 'learned his art from God'.

Exceptional though he was, Franz Schubert had to conform to school
rules. He wore the school uniform which consisted of a three-cornered
hat, a coat with a small epaulette on the left shoulder, a waistcoat, a
white cravat, knickerbockers and shoes with ornamental buckles; thus
attired, he and his friends walked through the streets in formation, like
boys of the Bluecoat school in Britain. He was required to excel not just

The school, run by his father, which Schubert attended until he was eleven

The school, run by his father, which Schubert attended until he was eleven

in music but in other subjects too, and Schubert did well in all respects. At the end of his second term at the Konvikt, his report read: 'Morals – good; Studies – good; Singing – very good; Viola – very good; Piano – very good. Remarks – a special musical talent.'

How fortunate for us that Schubert's education was not narrowly musical. At the Konvikt he was made aware of the great upsurge of romantic poetry from such masters as Goethe, Schiller, Klopstock, Rückert, Heine and Hölty. They wrote about love, happiness, sorrow, death and the beauty of the natural world in a way which moved the young Schubert intensely, so intensely that the words of such poets inspired him to become the greatest songwriter of all time. To some it is surprising that such a creator of songs should have come from Vienna, for the traditional home of German song hitherto had been cities such as Berlin and Hamburg in north Germany, the native soil of most of the romantic poets.

Also vastly important to Schubert's development were the friends he made at the Konvikt. The most important of these was Josef von Spaun, a young law student from Linz who was nine years older than Schubert. He was profoundly impressed when Franz first appeared in the orchestra as a newcomer to the second violins, and showed no

resentment when the boy subsequently replaced him at the leader's desk. They were to remain close friends for the rest of their lives.

Their friendship must have blossomed rapidly in Schubert's first year at the Konvikt, for Spaun left the school in 1809 and did not return to Vienna for two years. This created a problem for Schubert, because Spaun had kept him supplied with music paper. The supply ran out during Spaun's absence but was restored when he returned to Vienna. It seems that Schubert did not feel able to ask for supplies from home, as Spaun discovered quite early in their friendship. He recollected later:

> *Once, I found him alone in the music room, sitting at the piano. He was trying out a sonata by Mozart and said he liked it, but found Mozart very difficult to play. Encouraged by my friendly remarks, he played me a minuet of his own composition. He did it very shyly and blushed crimson but was pleased when I applauded him. He confided to me that he often expressed his secret thoughts in notes, but his father mustn't know, as he was absolutely against his devoting himself to music.*

Josef von Spaun, perhaps Schubert's truest friend

Among Schubert's other school friends were Albert Stadler, a pianist and composer who later became a barrister; Anton Holzapfel, a cellist and singer; Johann Michael Senn, a poet who played horn in the orchestra; and Georg Franz Eckel, who was to become a distinguished vet. To him we owe a description of the schoolboy Schubert as 'shy and uncommunicative, apt to spend his time alone in the music room, and walking along on school outings with lowered eyes and hands behind his back, completely absorbed in his own thoughts'.

The Konvikt was, like many schools, a self-contained community; the outside world on the whole made little impact on its life. There was a brief outbreak of patriotism in 1809 when Napoleon's army stood at the gates of Vienna and many of the older students rushed to join up, and in 1813 the grim realities of war were brought home to Schubert when his friend Theodor Körner fell in the battle of Gadebusch. Körner was resident poet at Vienna's Burgtheater from 1811 till his death in 1815, and had been brought into Schubert's life by Spaun. The sixteen-year-old Schubert was deeply affected by his death, setting some of Körner's martial texts to music and composing the 'Todesmusik' (later renamed 'Franz Schubert's Begrabnisfeier') in his honour.

Körner was not the only interesting person Schubert would encounter through Spaun's influence. Others were the poet and law student Johann Mayrhofer, and the well-to-do Franz von Schober, also a student of law, who was not a good influence on the composer, volatile as he was in the pursuit both of his profession and the opposite sex.

It was Spaun who, in 1811, after his return to the Konvikt, introduced the fourteen-year-old Schubert to the world of opera. The boy was moved to tears by Gluck's *Iphigenia in Tauris*; it led him to a study of all Gluck's scores. In 1814 Schubert sold some of his schoolbooks to buy a ticket for the première of the final version of Beethoven's *Fidelio*. Such experiences gave Schubert a driving ambition to succeed in the musical theatre. The first works he saw in Spaun's company were light pieces by Josef Weigl in the German *singspiel* tradition, combining music with spoken dialogue. These may have influenced the young composer when, in 1814 or thereabouts, he composed the first act of a magic opera called *Der Spiegelritter* (*The Looking-Glass Knight*) based on a play by August von Kotzebue. Though the music is tuneful and lively, it lacks any sense of drama, and *The Looking-Glass Knight* is the first indication that Schubert was a poor judge of theatrical librettos, a state of affairs quite at variance with his unerring ability to pick suitable texts for his songs.

The year 1812 was a watershed for Schubert. In May his mother Elizabeth died of 'nervous fever'. On 21 July it was announced that 'two boys in the Court Chapel, Franz Schubert and Franz Mullner, have suffered mutation of their voices'. An inscription in Schubert's own hand on an alto part of Peter Winter's first Mass reads: 'Schubert, Franz, crowed for the last time 26 July 1812'. But the breaking of a boy's voice did not mean that he had to leave the Konvikt. The relevant rule stated that choristers 'who distinguish themselves in their general behaviour and their studies are permitted, by order of the Emperor, to remain after their voices have broken'.

Antonio Salieri: he taught composition to Beethoven and Schubert

Schubert's early promise in areas other than music had not been maintained, for he had been spending most of his time composing and performing, but his music teachers spoke up for him and he was offered the Meerfeld endowment to enable him to stay on – provided his academic performance improved. Salieri took Schubert as his special pupil, giving him twice-weekly lessons in harmony and counterpoint. This was a real privilege, though not without its problems because, although Salieri had lived in Vienna since 1766, his German was punctuated with a good deal of French and Italian and, schooled as he was in the old Italian tradition, he had no interest in German romanticism or German song. But even so the arrangement seems to have worked reasonably well, and Salieri championed Schubert when, in the summer of 1813, the question of his continued free place at the Konvikt again came up for discussion. Salieri's word was enough to persuade the Emperor, who took a personal interest in the education of his choristers, to initial the proposal to safeguard Schubert's future when it was laid before him at his headquarters in the field before the battle of Leipzig. But since, as the document put it 'music and singing are but a subsidiary matter', Schubert was required

*Franz played viola in the
Schubert family string
quartet, here with the
addition of a double bass*

to take an examination after the summer to prove that he really was
capable of attaining the first grade in all subjects, including the dreaded
Latin and Mathematics. It was in these disciplines that, thanks to his
musical activities, Schubert's work had most conspicuously failed to
reach the required standard. There was a stormy scene at home.

Franz Schubert senior was a tough nut to crack, and when Schubert
junior had a problem making ends meet during his schooldays it was to
one of his elder brothers, probably Ignaz, that he wrote for help. 'The

few pence I get from father go to the devil in the first few days,' he wrote. 'What am I to do for the rest of the time? So what I thought was, how about letting me have a few shillings a month? You would never notice it, while I in my cell would think myself lucky and be satisfied.' The appeal was reinforced by a phoney Biblical quotation: 'Whosoever believeth in him shall not be ashamed' (Matthew: Chapter 3 verse 4).

But Schubert's schooldays were nearly over. There was no way he was prepared to treat music as a subsidiary matter. On 23 November 1813, he announced that he had given up his scholarship and would leave the Konvikt. There was no disgrace attached to his decision; far from it. His departure was marked by a school orchestra performance of his First Symphony, dedicated to the headmaster Dr Lang. Over the next few years Schubert played an active role in the musical life of the Konvikt, while continuing his lessons with Salieri.

Schubert had made peace with his father by composing a quartet for his name day, 27 September 1813, and now he decided to meet his father's wishes further by enrolling at a teacher-training college, the so-called Normal High School of St Anna. There is a suggestion that he did this to avoid military service, from which teachers were exempt, but at 4' 11" he was in any case below the minimum height for a soldier: this was just as well because the minimum period of military service was fourteen years! It is likely that Schubert thought teaching young children would prove less demanding of his time and attention than a rigorous academic education, and in this he was right. After his training he joined his brothers Ignaz and Ferdinand on the staff of their father's school. Until the autumn of 1816 he taught the elementary class for a token salary, but that had little to do with his real existence, for in that time he turned out a staggering total of 400 works including symphonies, five operas, string quartets, several masses and scores of songs.

Exceptionally talented composer though he was in his earlier years, Schubert was not a child prodigy in the Mozart or Mendelssohn league. His earliest works date from the year 1810, when he was thirteen (two fragmentary song sketches and a piano fantasia), and it wasn't until 1813 that he began to develop a style that was recognisably his own.

Mozart, Haydn and Beethoven were the strongest influences on his early style: we know that Mozart's Symphony No. 40 in G minor and Beethoven's Second Symphony were among his favourites; and he would also have been aware, thanks to the family string quartet, of the core chamber music repertoire of the classical period. Schubert wrote seven string quartets between 1810 and 1813, no doubt with the family in mind, and there were practical reasons for most of his other early pieces: sonatas and dances for his friends to play and choral music for the chapel choir. His earliest church music dates from around the time his voice broke in 1812. His models in this department were once again the classical masters, with special emphasis on the works of Joseph Haydn's brother Michael, to whom young Franz seems to have had a special devotion. When he was in Salzburg in 1825 he bypassed the Mozart landmarks to go straight to Michael Haydn's grave in St Peter's church, thus expressing his feeling towards that composer: 'There is no one on earth who admires you more than I do.'

At the age of fourteen in 1811, Schubert began to find his way into that territory which was to become so specially his musical home, the world of German song. When Spaun returned to the Konvikt in 1811, he found Schubert studying the songs of J. R. Zumsteeg (1760 – 1802) and in March 1811 the boy produced his own first song 'Hagars Klage' ('Hagar's Lament') which greatly impressed Salieri. Morbid sensationalism was one aspect of the romantic movement at this time (it was a popular vogue satirised by Jane Austen in *Northanger Abbey*) and several of Schubert's 1811 songs were in that vein. Among them was a setting of Schiller's 'Leichenfantasie' ('Corpse Fantasy'), which paints a gruesome picture of a father grieving at a moonlit funeral procession, and 'Der Vatermorder' ('The Parricide') with its insistent syncopated rhythm creating a powerful image of flight. These songs now seem to us almost ludicrously melodramatic, but they contain elements which Schubert's developing genius would forge into that timeless masterpiece of 1815, 'The Erlking'. This was one of the most sensational products of his first great creative period.

. III .

The Young Master

Schubert's training as a teacher did not distract him from his true occupation. So headlong was his approach to composition, he scarcely seems to have bothered about whether his work was performed or not, and perhaps this was just as well where his work for the theatre was concerned. Since he had completed no more than the first act of *The Looking-Glass Knight*, theatre managers were naturally not eager to produce the piece: it had to wait until 1949 for a performance – on the radio – in Switzerland.

Nor did Schubert's second theatre piece, *Der Teufels Lustschloss* (*The Devil's Pleasure Palace*) fare much better. It was not heard in public until 1879, when a concert performance was given in the Musikverein. Schubert started work on this operetta, based on another Kotzebue fairy-tale, almost as soon as he left the Konvikt. Its hero has to undergo a series of testing trials at his father-in-law's magic castle, a scenario that recalls Mozart's *Magic Flute*. The piece offered scope for spectacular scenic effects, and Schubert no doubt hoped these would appeal to a popular audience. There seems to have been an element of irony in Kotzebue's far-fetched saga, but this eluded Schubert, as did any trace of effective drama, except perhaps in the overture which is

Franz Schubert aged about sixteen, in a drawing by his friend Kupelwieser

still sometimes performed. Uncertain of what he had achieved, Schubert showed the first draft of the operetta to Salieri and subsequently rewrote the final act. But still no hope of a performance emerged.

However, the year 1814 did bring a measure of public success to Schubert: in October that year his Mass No. 1 in F for soloists, chorus and full orchestra with trombones was performed at a special service to mark the centenary of the church of Liechtenthal where, as a boy, Schubert had led the trebles in the choir. His brother Ferdinand played the organ and Schubert himself conducted in the presence of a congregation which included the entire parish of Liechtenthal and many notables, among them Salieri. Everyone loved the Mass, so much so that it was given again ten days later at the Augustiner church in the middle of Vienna. Schubert's father is said to have been so delighted that he gave his son a piano of his own.

Throughout his life Schubert continued to compose for the church: it was in those days one of the most important sources of patronage for a composer. But Schubert, like his brother Ignaz, had no patience with the more superstitious kinds of church ritual. A letter from Ignaz to Franz in October 1818 shows that they shared similar opinions on these matters. Describing a service held on a certain Saint's day, Ignaz wrote: 'At the end there was singing, and a relic of the Saint was given to all present to kiss, whereupon I noticed that several of the grown-ups crept out at the door, having no desire to share in this privilege.' Obviously the ideas of Ignaz and Franz were at variance with those of their father, because Ignaz added: 'If you should wish to write to Papa and me at the same time, do not touch upon any religious matters.' Replying a few days later to Ignaz alone, from the country home of the Esterházy family where he was employed as a tutor, Schubert declared: 'Your implacable hatred of the whole tribe of big-wigs does you credit. You have no conception of what a gang the priesthood is here: bigoted as mucky old cattle, stupid as arch-donkeys and boorish as bisons.' Such sceptical views make it unsurprising that the words in the Creed expressing belief in one

Holy, Catholic and Apostolic Church ('unam Sanctam, Catholicam et Apostolicam Ecclesiam') are missing from the Mass in F, as they are from Schubert's other settings of the Mass. The composer's agnostic attitude was well known to his friends, one of whom began a letter in 1827: 'Credo in unum Deum . . .' and went on: 'I know very well that you don't.' This perhaps helps to explain the fact that, with some notable exceptions, Schubert's church music fails to achieve the level of inspiration to be found elsewhere in his work.

If the success of his Mass in F was gratifying to Schubert as a first sign of public recognition, it was also significant for a more personal reason, for it brought him close to the girl who was probably the only great love of his life. Therese Grob was the soprano soloist in both performances of the Mass. Franz had known her since childhood, for their families were linked in friendship, but during rehearsals for the Mass, their relationship changed; over the next two years Schubert became passionately devoted to Therese, and there is little doubt he wanted to marry her. It appears that either Therese did not fully reciprocate Schubert's feelings, or her mother thought she could find something better than a poor schoolmaster for a husband. Whatever the reason, in 1816 they went their separate ways, Therese taking with her a parting gift from Franz of seventeen songs. In 1820 she married a wealthy baker.

But in the autumn of 1814 life must have looked hopeful to the seventeen-year-old Schubert in at least some respects. If so, his feelings would have been in tune with a widespread, if strictly temporary, sense of euphoria in the city of Vienna as a whole. The powers that be were assembled in the city for a Congress to settle the shape of Europe in the wake of what seemed the final defeat of Napoleon (the escape from Elba and Waterloo were still to come). The lands lost from the Austrian Empire had been restored, Metternich had not yet set up his secret army of spies, and Vienna seemed a wonderful place to be. As part of the celebrations, two huge Beethoven concerts were held in the Imperial Riding School on 29 November and 2 December 1814, with audiences of over 6,000 people. The programme gave the

Therese Grob in later life. Schubert was in love with her as a young girl

Viennese public the kind of musical festivity they craved. Apart from the Seventh Symphony, there was the specially composed cantata 'Der glorreiche Augenblick' ('The Glorious Moment') and that predecessor of the 1812 overture, the Battle Symphony.

Did Schubert attend one of those concerts? We know he was present in May 1814 at the first performance of the final version of *Fidelio*, and we know that he was only too well aware of Beethoven's dominant position in Viennese musical life at the time. 'After Beethoven,' he once asked, 'who can achieve anything more?' Was it because he felt over-awed that he avoided personal contact with the older master? There's no firm evidence that they ever met: only after Beethoven's death did Schubert feel strong enough to confront him, as one of the torch-bearers at his funeral.

Schubert's attitude towards Beethoven's music was ambivalent. He was certainly one of the major influences, together with Mozart and Haydn, on Schubert's symphonies from the early ones through to No. 9, the 'Great' C major which was intended to challenge Beethoven's grand style. But Schubert was not in sympathy with what he felt to be the wildness and perversity of some of Beethoven's later works. In a diary entry of 1816 which undoubtedly points at Beethoven, Schubert writes of:

> *that eccentricity which seems to prevail amongst the majority of present-day composers and for which one of our greatest German artists is responsible . . . there is no place for this eccentricity — an eccentricity which unites in indistinguishable confusion the heroic with the hideous, the hallowed with the Harlequin; which induces transports of frenzy instead of transports of delight, which provokes laughter instead of exalting men to God.*

(Schubert himself fell victim to such an accusation when, in 1823, a critic accused him of eccentricity in the *Rosamunde* music!)

If Schubert was overwhelmed by Beethoven, he quite simply loved Mozart. 'As from afar,' he confided to his diary in the summer of

Vienna's New Market and Palace

1816, after hearing one of Mozart's string quintets, 'the magic notes of Mozart's music still gently haunt me. These fair impressions . . . show us in the darkness of this life a light, clear and lovely, for which we confidently hope. O Mozart, immortal Mozart, how many, how endlessly many beneficent intimations of a better life have you imprinted on our souls!'

As soon as Schubert returned home from the Konvikt he started on a new work for the family string quartet – the quartet No. 8 in E Flat, the composer's longest and most impressive chamber music piece thus far. Then, by inviting former schoolfriends and others to join the quartet, he turned it into a small chamber orchestra which could play four-part arrangements of Haydn symphonies as well as some of Schubert's own compositions. When the orchestra outgrew the schoolroom, it moved first to the house of a city merchant, Franz Frischling. Later, in 1815, having acquired a wind section and drums, the orchestra moved to the house of the professional violinist Otto Hatwig who took over as leader. Schubert played the viola. It was a semi-amateur orchestra, but at least it gave Schubert the chance to try

A cameo of the young
Schubert by Theer

out some of his orchestral works. He wrote his symphonies Nos 2 to 5 between 1814 and 1818 for that group of musical friends.

The First in D, premièred by the Konvikt orchestra in October 1813, is a cheerful work with a *ländler*-like Trio to the Minuet and a bustling finale; the Second in B Flat shows hints of Beethoven's influence and has darker moments prophetic of Schubert's later compositions; the Third in D is full of vivacity and has a brilliant Rossinian last movement. The Fourth Symphony in C minor is in quite a different vein. Schubert himself gave it the title 'Tragic' and was clearly aware of Beethoven's epic Fifth Symphony and the String Quartet Op. 18 No. 4 in the same key, as well as Mozart's symphony No. 40 in G minor. Schubert's Fifth Symphony in B flat is an entirely successful essay in genial style for a rather smaller orchestra; maybe at that time in 1816 there were absentees from the ensemble at Otto Hatwig's house, or maybe Schubert deliberately set out to be more Mozartian than Beethovenian in the light of his diary comments that summer. The Sixth Symphony in C, completed in February 1818, was again on a larger scale; indeed Schubert labelled it 'Grosse Sinfonie' ('Grand Symphony'), and Beethoven's influence is once again evident, for example, in the choice of a Scherzo rather than a Minuet for the third movement. In addition, the spirit of Rossini haunts the piece in its Italianate exuberance. Whether Schubert heard his Sixth Symphony performed we don't know: none of the first six symphonies were made known to the wider world until their publication in the mid 1880s.

During his teaching years Schubert had access to the orchestra referred to above. He was even more dependent on his piano, an instrument which was undergoing rapid development, with some 135 keyboard instrument makers active in Vienna alone. From about 1811, the pianos of Nanette Streicher and Konrad Graf were equipped with pedals rather than knee-levers to modify the tone, and they opened up new possibilities of expressive playing.

Schubert himself was a competent pianist, but by no means a virtuoso, and this is surely one of the reasons why he never produced a full-scale concerto for that (or any other) instrument. He preferred to use the piano in more intimate domestic settings, where he took a modest pride in his ability to play, if not brilliantly, at least with true feeling, as a letter of 1825 makes clear. 'Several people', he informed his father after performing one of his piano sonatas, 'assured me that my fingers had transformed the keys into singing voices. If this is really true, then I am truly delighted, since I cannot abide the damnable thumping which is peculiar to even the most distinguished pianists and which pleases neither the ear nor the mind.'

Note the phrase 'singing voices' in that passage. In *Grand Piano*, Sidney Harrison comments that in performing Schubert melodies, one must play them 'as though one knew the non-existent words'. Schubert's output for solo piano and piano duet embraces great sonatas and other major works alongside slighter works and some 400 published keyboard dances (let alone the ones he improvised and never wrote down). But it was in the sphere of song more than any other that the piano in Schubert's hands found new significance.

We rightly think of Schubert's creation of over 600 songs as astonishing, but he was not the first composer of German songs to notch up a large score. J. R. Zumsteeg (1760–1802), whose works we know Schubert studied, turned out over 300 and J. F. Reichardt (1752–1814) no fewer than 1,500. What Schubert did was to weld the vocal line and the piano accompaniment into an instrument of infinite flexibility and emotional power, as the first exponent of a type of German *lied*, which would later call forth some of the finest and most beloved creations of Schumann, Brahms, Mahler, Hugo Wolf and Richard Strauss among others. Besides which, these *lieder* played an influential role in countless thousands of drawing-room ballads, in the days when the parlour piano was the centre of social activity in the home.

Schubert had only just finished his operetta *The Devil's Pleasure Palace* with its inadequate libretto when his reading led him to Goethe's *Faust*. There he found inspiration for his first masterpiece, the song 'Gretchen am Spinnrade' ('Gretchen at the Spinning

Wheel'). The song expresses Gretchen's anxiety and despair at being abandoned by Faust, and her ecstasy as she remembers happier times. The miracle of Schubert's setting is that he contrives to make the whirling piano accompaniment suggest both the motion of Gretchen's spinning wheel *and* her emotional mood of nervous distraction. The ability to create a picture and a state of mind at the same time is one of the hallmarks of Schubert as a songwriter.

Schubert composed 'Gretchen' on 19 October 1814, and in the next twelve months would set nearly thirty Goethe poems. Schubert admired that great man from afar (as he did Beethoven). He also

Schubert's manuscript score of 'Gretchen'

found lyrics for many of his songs closer to home, setting the work of poets in his own circle of friends. Through the agency of Josef von Spaun, he was introduced in 1824 to Johann Mayrhofer, whose words prompted some of Schubert's finest creations; on 3 December 1814 he composed his first Mayrhofer song, 'Am See' ('By the Lake').

The year 1815 has often been described as Schubert's 'annus mirabilis', the most prolific year of his life. Obsessed by the ideas which came to him in profusion, he would even compose in a class-room full of children. There's the almost certainly apocryphal tale of a sweetheart who left Schubert in later years in revenge for the punishment she'd received at his hands when she was in his class at school. 'It's quite true,' Schubert is said to have admitted. 'Her little gang would annoy me so much that the ideas went out of my head. Naturally I gave them a good beating – and now I have to suffer for it!'

By one means or another, in 1815 Schubert composed his Second
and Third symphonies, four operas, two masses, a string quartet in G
minor, various dances and sonata movements for piano and about
150 songs; twenty-eight were completed in August alone, among
them Goethe's 'Heidenröslein' ('The Hedge Rose') about a boy who
carelessly plucks a hedge rose and is duly scratched in return.
October saw the composition of twenty-four songs including a
Goethe setting which rapidly became Schubert's best-known song,
'Erlkönig'. It's the story of a father's frantic ride through the forest
with his sick child in his arms, pursued by Death in the guise of the
Erlking, who at the end claims the child for his own. The accompaniment is another fine example of Schubert's ability to suggest a visual
image and a psychological state at the same time. Largely composed

*Manuscript copy of
'Erlkönig', with its
daunting accompaniment*

of octave triplets played at the speed of a galloping horse, it presents notorious difficulties to pianists, who perhaps can take comfort from the fact that the composer himself found the triplets too difficult. The manuscript of a simpler version in the composer's hand does exist — perhaps it's the one he used himself.

It was said by Spaun that Schubert composed 'Erlkönig' in a lightning flash of inspiration. It's true that he wrote it out in a single afternoon; but he may have had Goethe's poem in mind for days if not longer, and he did produce four versions before he was satisfied. However, 'Erlkönig' quickly became very popular among Schubert's friends.

Unfortunately, not all of Schubert's friends served the composer well. For three months in 1815, Schubert worked on an operetta based on a Goethe libretto called *Claudine von Villa Bella*. The manuscript was given after Schubert's death to Josef Hüttenbrenner,

Johann Mayrhofer, who committed suicide in 1836

whose servants used Acts 2 and 3 to light a fire, so only the first act has survived. Josef and his brother Anselm were also involved in the disappearance of the 'Unfinished' Symphony.

In 1815, at the age of eighteen, Schubert was becoming the focal point of a circle of friends headed by his well-established mentor Josef von Spaun. They met sometimes at the Konvikt, where Schubert continued to play in the orchestra and attend musical evenings; and they gathered in Vienna's cafés to drink wine and discuss the arts and politics. Anselm Hüttenbrenner joined the group in 1815 when he came to Vienna for composition lessons with Salieri, who continued to be Schubert's teacher until 1817. From Anselm we have a comment about Schubert's indifference to social convention: 'Dress was a thing in which he took no interest whatever. He disliked bowing and scraping, and listening to flattering talk about himself he found downright nauseating.'

He got none of that from Johann Mayrhofer, who was described as 'taciturn and sarcastic'. His pessimistic nature led to two suicide attempts, the second of them, in 1836, successful. Mayrhofer's preoccupation with the darker side of life corresponded with a strong melancholy streak in Schubert, however much he might disguise it in company, and the two men were close friends, sharing rooms for two years from the autumn of 1818.

Another congenial spirit was Franz von Schober; a law student at the time he joined the circle in 1815, he later became private secretary to Franz Liszt and a chamberlain at the court of Weimar. So often were Schober and Schubert seen together at one stage that they were known collectively as 'Schobert'. Brilliant, theatrical and charming, Schober is said to have been instrumental in Schubert's involvement with a prostitute which led to his venereal infection. Schober also provided the lyrics for one of Schubert's most moving songs, 'An die Musik' (1817), which speaks of music leading to 'a better world' and opening the way to 'better times'.

Perhaps Schober had Schubert's role among his friends in mind when he wrote those lines; he would certainly have understood the sentiment expressed in a letter to him from Mayrhofer in September 1816: 'Today Schubert is coming to me and several friends; the mists of the present time, which are somewhat leaden, must be lifted by his melodies.' That same month, Mayrhofer wrote a poem for Schubert which expresses gratitude for his friend's ability to 'summon a heaven from the troubles of the present time'. Schubert returned the compliment by setting the poem to music – 'Geheimnis' ('Secret'). The composer shared Mayrhofer's view that the artist alone can find happiness in this world, since happiness is only possible through the creation of art.

Franz von Schober

In the poem 'Am Strome' ('By the Stream'), which Schubert set in March 1817, Mayrhofer compares life's journey to a river:

> Flow onward to the distant sea;
> Not for you to feel at home here.
> I too long for kinder shores,
> Finding no joy on earth.

A preoccupation with death as a source of release from the troubles of this life was common among Romantic poets, and as a result many of Schubert's songs explore that theme, most notably perhaps 'Death and the Maiden' (1817) where Death appears in the poem by Claudius as a friend who is coming not to punish the maiden but to soothe her so that in his arms she may gently sleep.

While his friends found consolation in listening to his music, Schubert himself was encouraged by a growing entourage of admiring supporters. In addition to Spaun, Schober and Mayrhofer, they included the politically active radical Johann Senn; the scholar Franz von Bruchmann, who steered Schubert's attention towards great literary works; the playwright Eduard von Bauernfeld; and the artist and illustrator Moritz von Schwind. Von Schwind's drawing 'A Schubert Evening at Spaun's' gives an impression of a Schubertiad in progress, with more than the inner circle of friends in attendance to enjoy it. 'Happy moments brighten this gloomy

A Schubertiad with Kupelwieser and others in elegant surroundings

life,' wrote Schubert in his diary 'and happier ones give glimpses of happier worlds.'

Like so many artists of that Romantic era, the young composer felt a deep affinity with nature. Not nature drilled into submission as in the formal gardens of Versailles or Schönbrunn, but nature wild and untamed, in the natural state, the way Beethoven saw it in the 'Pastoral' Symphony. 'There can be scarcely anything more agreeable,' wrote Schubert, 'than to enjoy the green country on an evening after a hot summer's day, a pleasure for which the fields between Währing and Döbling seem to have been specially created. In the uncertain twilight and in the company of my brother Karl, my heart warmed within me.'

But, as many dramatic passages in his songs suggest, Schubert also responded to the awesome power of natural phenomena, as the contemporary painter Turner did in so many of his works, among them 'Fall of an Avalanche in Grisons' (1810).

In the eyes of the Romantics, human beings were just as capable of being racked by tempests as the natural world. Human suffering and sadness (only to be relieved by Death) were thus frequent subjects of the poems Schubert set to music. He certainly had his own share of unhappiness and knew the pangs of unrequited love, which would have given him a ready sympathy with, for example, Heine's 'Der

Döppelganger': the ghostly double who haunts the dwelling of a departed loved-one (the Romantics were just as fascinated by the supernatural as they were by the natural). But Schubert felt a wider sympathy for all who were rejected by the world, expressed at its most poignant in the last song of the *Winter Journey* cycle (1827), 'Der Leiermann' ('The Hurdy-Gurdy Man') which offers the image of a desolate figure grinding out tunes nobody wants to hear in an icily indifferent world. Already in the few pages that survive of the diary he started in 1816 we find him reflecting gloomily on the human situation. 'Man,' commented the nineteen-year-old in acceptably Romantic fashion, 'is a ball to be played with by chance and passion.'

Goethe: he was not interested in Schubert's many settings of his poems

Perhaps because he wanted to leave home, perhaps because he thought a steady job would give him a better chance of marrying Therese Grob, Schubert applied in April 1816 for a music master's job at a school in far-away Laibach (now Ljubljana). He failed to send in his application until two months after the post was advertised, which suggests that he didn't want it much and was probably relieved when it went to someone else. More promising hopes arose that April, when the good Spaun launched a scheme to publish Schubert's songs in a series of volumes, each devoted to a single poet. He sent twenty-eight Goethe settings to the poet himself, with the offer of a dedication to the man 'to whose glorious poetry [Schubert] is indebted for his development into a German songwriter'. Goethe returned the songs without comment; and when in 1825 Schubert published three of his Goethe songs with dedications to the poet, he again made no response. However, when Spaun's publishing hopes of 1816 were dashed, he invited Vienna's VIPs to musical evenings at his own house, thus offering another means by which Schubert's works could become more widely known.

The year 1816 was not quite so productive for Schubert as 1815 had been, but he did create over 100 songs, returning again to Goethe in the autumn of that year with settings of poems from *Wilhelm Meister* including songs of the Harper, a figure who embodies the Romantic image of the alienated artist. Also that autumn, to a poem by G. P. Schmidt of Lübeck, Schubert composed a song which was to rival 'Erlkönig' in popularity, 'Der Wanderer', which expresses all the Romantic longing for the unattainable: 'There, where you are not, only there is happiness.' The song later provided the basis of the *Wanderer Fantasy* for piano solo.

Schubert composed a good deal of church music in 1816 – an Offertory, a Stabat Mater, two settings of Salve Regina, a Tantum Ergo, a Magnificat and a Mass in C. He advanced to a new maturity in chamber music with the String Quartet No. 11 in E major and the three delightful piano and violin sonatas. Through 1815 and 1816 Schubert continued his efforts to win acceptance in the musical theatre, without success. The one-act comic operetta *Der Vierjährige Posten* (*The Four-Year Sentry-Go*) to a libretto by Theodor Körner finally reached the stage at Dresden in 1896; another one-act piece, *Fernando* (June – July 1815), with distant affiliations to Beethoven's *Fidelio*, was eventually produced in Vienna in 1907; what remained of the Goethe operetta *Claudine von Villa Bella* (June – September 1815) was seen in Vienna in 1913; *Die Freunde von Salamanka* (November – December 1815) to a lighthearted text by Mayrhofer, did not find an audience until 1928 in Halle; and *Die Bürgschaft* (*The Community*), of which only the first two acts were completed, ran into trouble with the censors because it dealt with the attempted assassination of a tyrant and had to wait for its première until 1908 in Vienna.

On 16 June 1816, Schubert shared the general joy at a concert to mark the fiftieth anniversary of the arrival of his teacher Salieri in Vienna. 'It must be a lovely and refreshing experience,' wrote Schubert in his diary, 'for an artist to see all his pupils gathered round him, while each of them gives of his best in honour of the occasion.' On 24 July there was a concert in honour of the name day of Professor Watteroth, a liberal activist and hero of the radical student movement. For this Schubert wrote his cantata *Prometheus*, a landmark because it brought Schubert his first tangible reward for composition.

'Today,' he noted in the diary for 17 June, 'I composed for money for the first time, namely a cantata for Professor Watteroth, words by Draxler. The fee is 100 florins.' We are not able today to judge the quality of *Prometheus* because the manuscript disappeared completely in 1828, but it seems to have been a success: a second performance with piano accompaniment was given in January 1819 at the house of Leopold Sonnleitner, who hosted influential musical evenings and did his best to advance Schubert's cause. Through Sonnleitner, the composer met the poet and dramatist Franz Grillparzer, who followed Schubert's career closely and was to write the epitaph on his tombstone.

Leopold Sonnleitner

Around December 1816 Schubert decided to escape from teaching and from the family home. He moved in with his friend Franz von Schober and began an existence as a freelance composer, without any of the opportunities Mozart and Beethoven had had when they arrived in Vienna to earn money by performing in public. He could have taken pupils but chose not to, sharing the view of the poet Novalis that genius should be absolved from moral and social obligations; in any case, for the moment he was welcome to enjoy the hospitality of the well-off Schober family. In a further bid for freedom, Schubert decided at the beginning of 1817 to sever his long association with Salieri who, according to Spaun, 'repeatedly took Schubert to task for occupying himself with poems in the barbarous German language'. Schubert had by then advanced much too far down that road to turn back at the command of an Italian kapellmeister, however well-regarded he was.

More than half of Schubert's total output of some one thousand works were completed by the time he reached his twentieth birthday in January 1817. That year Schubert worked on five piano sonatas, all of them influenced by Beethoven: two, the A minor and B major, were completed; three others in E minor, A Flat and D Flat were left unfinished. In addition, 1817 saw the production of some sixty songs, including Goethe's 'Ganymed', Schiller's 'Gruppe aus dem Tartarus' ('Scene from Hades'), 'Die Forelle' ('The Trout') to words by

Schubert, 'Der Tod und das Mädchen' to words by Claudius, Schober's 'An die Musik' and Mayrhofer's 'Memnon' and 'Am Strome'.

In the spring of 1817, Schubert and Spaun made another attempt to publish by sending 'Erlkönig' to Breitkopf and Härtel. The composer was so completely unknown to them that they returned the manuscript to another Franz Schubert who worked in Dresden as a composer and double-bass player. His reply reads as follows:

With the greatest astonishment I beg to state that this cantata was never composed by me. I shall retain the same in my possession in order to learn, if possible, who sent you that sort of trash in such an impolite fashion, and also to discover the fellow who has misused my name.

Johann Michael Vogl, fine singer and firm friend of Schubert

Fortunately for *the* Franz Schubert, 'Erlkönig' was about to become a great favourite with one of the leading singers of the day, who came into his life through the efforts of Schober. This was Johann Michael Vogl, the prestigious principal baritone at the Kärntnertor Theatre. Vogl took some persuading to meet the unknown young man, but when they did get together to try out some of Schubert's songs, Vogl rapidly graduated from half-hearted interest to whole-hearted enthusiasm. He did not at once suggest a second meeting, to the composer's disappointment, but after a few days he reappeared, having made up his mind to take Schubert's songs into his repertoire. 'The impression made on Vogl by the songs of Schubert was overwhelming,' wrote Spaun. 'He came frequently into our circle without being asked, invited Schubert to his house and studied songs with him. He now ranked among Schubert's most ardent admirers. It had been his intention before to give up music but now he was enamoured of it afresh.'

Vogl and Schubert, now often seen in each other's company, were physically an ill-assorted pair, with Vogl at over six feet towering above Schubert, but mentally and spiritually they were very much in tune. Both loved Goethe and the other Romantic poets and Schubert paid heed to the intelligent Vogl's musical ideas and critical comments. Vogl lamented the lack of a school of singing adequate to do justice to Schubert's creations; he was himself the first of a long line of singers down to the present time who would regard the interpretation of Schubert as one of the highest challenges of their profession.

In August 1817, Schubert's freedom had to end for a time when Schober's brother returned to Vienna on leave and needed to occupy the composer's accommodation. The only course open to Franz was to return home, and that meant more drudgery as a teacher. Things improved a little in December of that year when his father got a new job as headmaster, which brought with it a more spacious house nearer to the city centre. But Schubert's stepmother had a young family of her own, and it must have been hard for Franz to find a quiet corner to work. This perhaps accounts for the fact that he produced relatively little during the first half of 1818, with the exception of the 'Grand Symphony' No. 6 in C.

If that work had Rossinian traits, Schubert also had Rossini in mind when he wrote, in 1817, two overtures 'in the Italian style'. In March 1818 one of these became the first of Schubert's instrumental works to be played in public when it was included in a concert at a hotel which still stands in Vienna's Annagasse, Der Römische Kaiser (The Roman Emperor). Though the overture had to compete for attention with a child prodigy, the seven-year-old pianist Leopoldine Blahetka, it attracted a pleasing review in *Theaterzeitung* (*Theatre News*) which referred to 'a wondrously lovely overture by Herr Franz Schubert, a pupil of our much-venerated Salieri, who has already learned how to touch and convulse all hearts . . . it is to be wished that this artist will soon delight us with a new gift'. The same reviewer again praised the young composer's 'profound feeling, disciplined yet spontaneous force and appealing charm' when one of the Italian-style overtures was played at another concert by eight hands on two pianos, presumably doubling up Schubert's own four-hand version. There were more favourable

SCHLOSS ZELIZ

Postcard views of the Hungarian castle where Schubert spent two summers with the Esterházy family

reviews in Viennese and other newspapers when one of the overtures was given at another concert in Vienna at Müller's Hall; meanwhile, the Philharmonic Society announced a series of chamber music concerts at which music by Haydn, Mozart, Beethoven and Schubert was to be played, an indication that at least some people knew he was worthy of inclusion in such company. These encouraging signs belong to a year which also saw in February the publication of the very first Schubert song to appear in print: 'Erlafsee' ('Lake Erlaf'), a setting of words by Mayrhofer written in September 1817. It appeared in an anthology of prose and verse for lovers of the countryside advertised in the *Wiener Zeitung* (*Vienna News*).

Release from the renewed bondage of teaching (and from the family home) came in the summer of 1818 when Count Johann Karl Esterházy of Galanta invited Schubert to spend some months at his estate at Zseliz in Hungary (about 100 miles east of Vienna) as music

teacher to his two young daughters, Marie and Karoline. Schubert accepted without hesitation, duly applying for a travel permit for his first trip outside his native city.

Esterházy provided Schubert with a reasonable salary and rooms of his own (in the servants' quarters) at his castle set in beautiful countryside. All the Esterházy family could sing and Karoline was a good pianist, so the prospects seemed rosy. 'I am very well. I live and compose like a god,' said Schubert, in a letter of 3 August addressed to his friends Spaun, Schober, Mayrhofer and Senn. 'It was high time, otherwise I should have become just another thwarted musician.' Another letter to the friends dated 8 September described his surroundings:

Our castle is not one of the largest but very neatly built. It is surrounded by the most beautiful garden. I live in the Steward's

The music room at Zseliz. The Esterházy girls played the piano well, and Schubert was fond of them

Baron von Schönstein, a house-guest at Zseliz who could sing for his supper

quarters. It is fairly quiet except for about 40 geese which cackle so loudly sometimes that one cannot hear oneself speak. Good people around me, all of them . . . the Count is a bit rough, the Countess haughty but sensitive, and the young Countesses are nice children.

No wonder brother Ignaz envied Franz. 'You happy creature!' he wrote. 'You live in sweet, golden freedom and can give rein to your musical genius . . . you are loved, admired and idolised, while the likes of us wretched scholastic beasts of burden are abandoned to all the roughnesses of wild youngsters and exposed to a host of abuses.'

That was a reminder of what Schubert had left behind. The downside of life at Zseliz was that he felt cut off from the operatic scene in Vienna and isolated in other ways. 'I am obliged to rely wholly on myself. I have to be composer, author, audience and goodness knows what else. Not a soul here has any feeling for true art. So I am alone with my beloved [music] and have to hide her in my room, in my pianoforte and in my bosom.'

Since his main job was to give piano lessons at Zseliz, many of his compositions at the castle were for that instrument including a set of variations dedicated to Beethoven 'from his admirer and worshipper Franz Schubert', and the famous 'Marches Militaires' for piano duet.

Schubert was not altogether lacking in congenial company, for one of the house guests at Zseliz was the singer Baron Karl von Schönstein, who became one of Schubert's most enthusiastic supporters and a fine interpreter of his songs. There was also consolation in the presence of a chambermaid called 'Pepi' Pockelhofer, described by Schubert in his letters as 'very pretty and often my companion'. It's not known if they were lovers but they were certainly close friends, for Pepi visited Schubert in later years whenever she came to Vienna. Perhaps she helped him forget Therese.

By October whatever pleasures Zseliz offered were beginning to pall. 'If I did not get to know these people round me better every day, things would be just as good with me as at the beginning. But now I see that I am really lonely among them,' he wrote to brother

Ferdinand. 'My longing for Vienna grows daily. We shall be off by the middle of November.'

When the family returned to their winter residence in the Imperial city, Schubert continued giving lessons to those 'truly nice girls' as he called them, the two young Countesses, but he decided to make his home with Mayrhofer who lived on the third floor above a tobacconist's shop. There he composed all day and every day, though he did take time off in the evenings to spend time with his friends. One of them, Anselm Hüttenbrenner, who often visited Schubert, used to find him in a 'nearly dark, damp, unheated little room, huddled up in an old threadbare dressing-gown, freezing and composing'. Schubert said himself: 'I compose one piece and when I have finished one I immediately begin another.'

Quite often when a new idea seized him he would not complete the work in hand, but that winter he did finish the music for yet another theatre work, this time with a real prospect of production. The singer Michael Vogl had persuaded the management of the Kärntnertor Theatre to commission Schubert to write the music for a one-act farce called *Die Zwillingsbrüder* (*The Twin Brothers*). Schubert set to work at once and the score was ready on 19 January 1819.

. IV .

A Taste of Freedom

Although Michael Vogl, a big star in Vienna's musical firmament, was due to appear as both the twin brothers in *Die Zwillingsbrüder*, the management of the Kärntnertor Theatre thought their box office prospects would be better served if they stuck for the time being to Italian opera. So the production of *Die Zwillingsbrüder* was postponed for eighteen months, though Schubert did receive part of his promised fee of 500 florins by way of an advance.

Meanwhile, in the early months of 1819, Schubert was attracting attention in other ways. There was a further performance of the cantata 'Prometheus', composed in honour of the liberal Professor Watteroth, and on 28 February a Schubert recital by Franz Jäger at 'The Roman Emperor' drew the surprising compliment from a critic that Schubert's songs were 'most amusing'. 'Schäfers Klaglied' ('Shepherd's Lament') to words by Goethe was particularly enjoyed by another critic, though this sad account of lost love in a pastoral setting was hardly intended to raise a smile. In March there was a concert at Müller's Hall given by the Society of Amateurs which included an overture of Schubert's – perhaps the one in E minor written the previous month, a substantial piece which lacks Schubertian charm and is seldom heard nowadays.

*Schubert and Vogl, ill-
assorted physically but at
one in their love of music*

In July Schubert left his struggles for recognition in Vienna and set off with Michael Vogl to visit some of Vogl's friends in the country and to explore the mountains and lakes of Upper Austria. Did Schubert find it hard to keep up with his tall companion as they roamed the countryside? Known to his friends as 'Schwammerl' (Little Mushroom), he was, as the musical barrister Leopold Sonnleitner charitably put it, 'below average height'. Sonnleitner, like others, considered the water-colour portrait of Schubert painted a few years later (in 1825) by Wilhelm August Rieder to be the best likeness of the composer. In praising it, he added this vivid verbal picture of his own:

*Schubert had a round, fat face, a short neck and not too high a
forehead, a mass of brown and naturally curly hair, round shoulders
and back, chubby arms and hands with short fingers, and, if I
remember rightly, grey-blue eyes. Bushy brows, nose short and wide
and thick lips; his face was rather Moorish. His head was hunched
between his shoulders and pushed forward. He always wore glasses.
His expression was obtuse more than intellectual and inclined to be
sullen. Only if he was observed more closely while listening to music
or engaged in interesting conversation did his face become more alive,
his mouth smiling, his eyes sparkling and his whole posture more
relaxed.*

There was plenty to make Schubert smile as he and Vogl settled down
after their strenuous days to enjoy evenings of feasting and music at
the houses of Vogl's friends in his home town of Steyr. There were
other attractions too. 'In the house where we are staying', Schubert
told Mayrhofer in a letter, 'there are eight girls, nearly all of them
pretty. So you see we have something to do.' Among the families
which entertained the friends were the Schellmanns and the Stadlers,
the Paumgartners and the Köllers. Mayrhofer was informed that 'Von
Köller's daughter [Josephine] is very pretty too and plays the piano
excellently'. For Josephine, Schubert composed his lyrical and serene
Piano Sonata in A major (D664).

The Paumgartner household also provided musical stimulus, for
Sylvester Paumgartner was an able cellist whose income as a mining
engineer enabled him to commission a new work from Schubert: it
turned out to be a quintet for piano and strings. Schubert compli-
mented his patron by giving the cello a rewarding share of melody,
assigning the less interesting bottom line to a double bass; and he
adopted Paumgartner's suggestion of using the song 'Die Forelle' as
the basis of a variation movement. The song also provided the work
with its nickname: the 'Trout' Quintet (D667). It has become one of
the composer's most beloved creations, reflecting as it surely does
the untroubled happiness of those summer months in the Austrian

countryside. Vogl and Schubert also visited Linz and there were unrealised plans to continue to Salzburg.

In the course of 1819 Schubert found time to produce about thirty songs, drawing inspiration from Romantic poets new to him as well as his favourites. One was Friedrich von Schlegel, critic, philosopher and acknowledged leader of Vienna's circle of Romantic writers. In February 1819 Schubert created the first of his twelve settings of lines from Schlegel's *Abendröte* (*Sunsets*), a sequence of poems about the presence of God in nature: no doubt Schubert would have been in sympathy with Schlegel's view that the deity was more likely to be encountered in the open air than in the established church. From nature Schubert turned to the subject of death as explored in *Hymns to the Night* by the death-obsessed and short-lived Friedrich Leopold von Hardenberg (1772–1801) who wrote under the pseudonym Novalis. One of Schubert's most successful Novalis settings was 'Marie' (1819), a love song to the Virgin Mary.

While experimenting with new poets, Schubert continued to set those he had already come to admire. In October 1819 he returned to Goethe, setting 'Prometheus' and (for the second time) 'An den Mond' ('To the Moon'). In the same month he set another four poems by his friend Mayrhofer, including 'Die Sternenächte' ('Starry Nights') and 'Nachtstück' ('Night Piece').

While he was in Linz during the summer, he had ended a letter to Mayrhofer with the question: 'Have you done anything yet? I hope so.' The query probably referred to an operatic project the pair of them had in mind, based on a story from classical antiquity about Prince Adrastus. When Schubert returned to Vienna in the autumn of 1819 he worked on the score, but nothing survives of it except eight numbers and a few sketches.

Some of the most beautiful dramatic music Schubert ever wrote went into the incomplete *Lazarus*, an Easter cantata on the story in St John's Gospel of Lazarus, raised from the dead by Jesus. This religious drama was planned to deal in three acts with the death, burial and miraculous resurrection of Lazarus, and was probably

*The German writer and poet Johann Wolfgang von Goethe
(1749–1832), relaxing in the Rome countryside. Goethe was one of
Schubert's principal inspirations.*

'The Red Crayfish', the house in north-west Vienna where Schubert
was born in January 1797. It is now a museum.

An early portrait of the composer.

The story of Schubert has been greatly romanticised over the years.
Here and on subsequent pages, we see images of Franz which suggest
little of the ultimate tragedy of his life.

intended – indeed may have been commissioned – for performance during Lent when the Viennese theatres were closed; but Schubert got no further than the middle of the second act.

Schubert was apt to abandon a piece of work when he lost interest, or lost confidence in his ability to complete it, but it's possible that his failure to finish *Lazarus* was connected with his involvement in a police raid.

In March 1819, the dramatist August von Kotzebue, who, though popular as a writer, was hated for his repressive views and suspected of being a government agent, was assassinated by a young student. On this cue, Metternich's police stepped up their surveillance of all suspicious individuals, especially in the student community.

Johann Senn, who was banished by Metternich's thought-police

By March 1820, Vienna had become a very uncomfortable place for anyone with liberal sympathies, and when, in that month, Schubert, Franz von Bruchmann and others got together at the home of Johann Senn, already known for his rebellious attitude, the police decided to storm the house and submit the whole party to questioning.

The incident was described in a police report:

Concerning the stubborn and insulting behaviour evinced by Johann Senn on the occasion of the examination and confiscation of his papers carried out by regulation in his lodgings, during which he used the expressions, among others, that he 'did not care a hang about the police' and further that 'the Government was too stupid to be able to penetrate into his secrets'. It is also said that his friends who were present [including] Schubert, the school assistant from the Rossau, chimed in against the authorised official in the same tone, inveighing against him with insulting and opprobrious language . . . The Chief Constable observes that this report will be taken into account during the proceedings against Senn; moreover, those individuals who have conducted themselves rudely . . . during the visit to Senn will be called and severely reprimanded.

Senn, who was the only one of the group to be detained, paid a heavy price for his fearlessness. He languished in jail without charge for fourteen months and was then deported to his native Tyrol, his career in ruins. Schubert never saw him again, though in September 1822 Bruchmann visited Senn and brought back two of his poems for Schubert to set.

The only man in Vienna who could, it seemed, say what he liked about the Establishment and get away with it was Ludwig van Beethoven, either because his artistic status made him unassailable or, more likely, because the authorities regarded him as a raving lunatic.

But Schubert was lucky too. Apparently he emerged from his involvement in the Senn incident with nothing worse than a black eye. Metternich could easily have banned his stage works from the theatres of Vienna. Instead, on 14 June 1820, the curtain at last rose on a Schubert opera – although not a full-scale opera. Described as 'A Farce with Songs in One Act' (nothing seditious there) *The Twin Brothers* ran for a reasonably respectable six performances at the Kärntnertor Theatre.

One of those present on the first night was Mozart's son Franz Xaver Wolfgang. He noted in his diary that 'this little operetta with music by Herr Schubert, a beginner, contains some quite pretty things, but is a little too serious'. Though some of those present hissed the new piece, Schubert's friends, according to a member of the audience, 'made a lot of noise: at the close there was a fuss until Vogl appeared and said "Schubert is not present – I thank you in his name"'. In fact Schubert *was* there, but flatly refused to take a bow; afterwards he went off to celebrate with friends at Lenkay's wine bar.

He had reason to be pleased with the newspaper reviews in general, though they were not what you'd call rave notices. 'The general verdict on Schubert can only be favourable,' said Vienna's *Conversationsblatt*, 'though not to the point to which his numerous friends endeavour to force it. He will do great and beautiful things, and it is in this hope that we welcome the modest artist very cordially.' There was coverage as far afield as Dresden and Leipzig, which in itself was encouraging. However, the Dresden paper, while admitting that Schubert was 'a gifted young man', objected because 'the public acclaimed the operetta like a great masterpiece, which it is not'; and the Leipzig critic warned Schubert not to get above himself: 'In this first dramatic essay he seems to attempt to fly as high as Beethoven and not to heed the warning example of Icarus. Little true songfulness is to be found, whereas hardly any repose is to be met with in confused and surcharged instrumentation, anxious striving after originality and continual modulation.'

The critic of Vienna's *Allgemeine Musikalische Zeitung*, while rather more generous to the young composer's talents, took a similar line and offered plausible reasons for Schubert's ultimate failure as an opera composer:

> *Herr Schubert . . . has so far been known to us only by a few meritorious romances; his opera . . . attests its composer as a gifted mind, full of force and invention — a major advantage since everything else can be acquired . . . the music for* The Twin Brothers *has much originality and many interesting passages . . . but it is a blot on the work that the sentiments of simple country folk are interpreted much too seriously . . . comic music does not take at all kindly to a very close adherence to the words, or to the composer's taking refuge in a modulation whenever pain, for instance, is mentioned . . . Herr Schubert is too much wedded to details of the text, and this chases him and his hearer restlessly through modulations and allows of no point of repose; he tries to express words in music instead of painting the nature of a whole speech by means of the character of a whole piece.*

In other words, Schubert approached his libretti in the same way as he approached his song texts, unwilling to let a word go until he'd found the best possible way of expressing its meaning in music. Thus he was apt to lose sight of the broad sweep of his dramatic texts, treating

Vienna's Theater an der Wien

every aria and chorus as though it were a drama in itself rather than part of a larger pattern.

Despite some adverse comment, Schubert's reputation was certainly growing, and at about the same time as *The Twin Brothers* opened, he became involved in another stage project. The Theater an der Wien required a new opera to use at a benefit performance for the theatre's designer, technician and costumier. It seems the name of Schubert had already come up in discussion, and the designer Hermann Neefe asked his relative-by-marriage Leopold von Sonnleitner for his advice. The result was that Schubert was commissioned, and completed the piece in a few weeks, ready for performance on 19 August 1820.

This was the fairy-tale opera *Die Zauberharfe* (*The Magic Harp*), adapted from the French by the librettist of *The Twin Brothers*, Georg von Hofmann. Schubert's friend Franz von Schlechta described it as 'two parts sorcery, one good, one evil; a moonstruck lady in a ruined castle; an enraged father and a banished son; some foolish knights; a bucketful of tears; a handful of sighs and a stiff dose of the most nonsensical magic'. Once again Schubert's music, described by Vienna's *Conversationsblatt* as 'wonderfully beautiful' had to battle against a dreadful book, but the composer got his share of the blame for the failure of the piece. 'On the whole,' said Leipzig's main musical journal, '[the score] lacks technical resource and wants the confidence that only experience can give. Most of it is much too long, ineffective and fatiguing.' Once again the Vienna *Theaterzeitung* tried to be kind.

> *It is to be wished that the composer will in future find a better subject: nothing very edifying can be said about the book of this melodrama . . . eagle and doves, genii and monsters appear — all in vain, for there is no entertainment. Everything is left to the music, the settings and the machines. Yet even these united forces are incapable of overcoming a flood of boredom.*

One might think that Schubert by now would have been on his guard where librettos were concerned, but in October 1820 he embarked on another unpromising magic opera with a book derived from Indian mythology. The score never got further than sketches for the first two acts, and *Sakuntala* became yet another Schubert opera that never was.

Schubert's interest in an Indian subject may have arisen from his meeting with a leading orientalist at the house of the poet Matthäus von Collin, who did all he could at that time to introduce Schubert to Vienna's most influential figures in the arts, including the head of the Imperial music establishment, Count Dietrichstein; the author Karoline Pichler, who presided over a prestigious salon; and the Patriarch of Venice, Ladislaus Pyrker, who was also a poet.

Against Schubert's acquisition of important friends must be set the decisive loss of the girl he'd once hoped to wed (Therese Grob married the master baker Johann Bergmann in November 1820) and the dissolution of the private orchestra which had given him the chance to hear some of his own early works, as well as masterpieces by other great composers such as Handel, Haydn and Beethoven. The reason for this sad development was that the owner of the house where the orchestra rehearsed won first prize in a lottery and decided forthwith to sell up in Vienna and settle in the country on the proceeds.

*The title page of
'Erlkönig', published with
financial help from
Schubert's friends*

But by way of consolation, the prosperous Ignaz Sonnleitner offered his own house for private fortnightly concerts of Schubert's works. There, on 1 December 1820, August Gymnich sang 'Erlkönig' to a very enthusiastic audience. Sonnleitner decided the song must become known to a wider public, and clubbed together with a few friends to pay for the publication of the song by the firm of Cappi and Diabelli. The first print-run of 100 copies sold out within days: by September 1821, 800 copies had been printed and by the end of that year a total of twenty Schubert songs had been published.

Towards the end of 1820, Schubert decided to move out from Mayrhofer's rooms and find lodgings of his own nearby. His painter friend Schwind made a drawing of the composer's room – complete with piano. Here, in December 1820, Schubert began work on a string quartet in C minor which got no further into the second movement than a 41-bar sketch. But the completed first movement is in itself a masterpiece. It has come down to us as the 'Quartettsatz' ('Quartet Movement'), and it ranks among the composer's most dramatic and compelling chamber music compositions. Also in that

*Schwind's drawing of
Schubert's room*

month of December, Schubert set poems by Schlegel and Mayrhofer
as well as creating one of his most appealing part songs, a setting for
women's voices of Psalm 23.

If widespread publication was slow in coming to Schubert, critical
appreciation of his merits as a song composer was growing. On 30
January 1821, the *Dresden Evening News* had this to say:

> *The young composer Schubert has set to music several songs by the best
> poets, which testify to the profoundest studies combined with genius
> worthy of admiration, and attract the eyes of the cultivated musical
> world. He knows how to paint in sound, and the songs 'The Trout',
> 'Margaret at the Spinning Wheel' . . . and 'The Combat' by Schiller,*

surpass in characteristic truth all that may be found in the domain of song.

The publication of 'Gretchen am Spinnrade' in May 1821 was greeted with a perceptive review in the Vienna *Sammler*: 'Margaret's state of mind, in which the feelings and sensations of love, of pain, and of rapture take turns, are so affectingly depicted by Schubert's music that a more heart-stirring impression than that left by his musical picture is scarcely imaginable.'

The same month there was a newspaper comment on the piano part of 'Erlkönig' which will strike a chord with any pianist who has tried it:

> *One could wish that Herr Schubert had occasionally transferred [the triplet accompaniment] to the left hand and thus facilitated performance; for the ceaseless striking of one and the same note in triplets throughout whole bars tires the hand, if the piece is to be taken at the rapid pace demanded by Herr Schubert.*

Such comments reflect the interest aroused by the gradual appearance in print of Schubert's songs, and the fact that in the first four months of 1821, no fewer than thirteen public concerts featured performances of the songs by such artists as Vogl and Gymnich. On 25 January, to take one example, Gymnich sang 'Erlkönig' at a Philharmonic Society concert, and the following evening the weekly Schubertiad at Schober's was extremely festive. There were fourteen people present, among them a certain Josef Huber, who described the occasion in a letter to his fiancée:

> *A lot of splendid songs by Schubert were sung and played by himself, which lasted until after ten o'clock in the evening. After that punch was drunk, offered by one of the party, and as it was good and plentiful the party, in happy mood already, became even merrier; so it was three o'clock in the morning before we parted.*

A Schubertiad hosted by Spaun

As Schubert became better known, the Schubertiad became an increasingly fashionable way to spend an evening in Vienna. Apart from singing or accompanying his songs, he would often sit at the piano for hours improvising dances for the assembled company. He wrote some of them down (waltzes, écossaises, etc.) and a collection of his dances was published before any of his other instrumental works.

Schubert was by no means the only serious composer who wrote dance music at that time. Early in 1821 the publisher Antonio Diabelli invited fifty or so composers to write a variation each on a waltz of his own creation. Schubert and the ten-year-old Franz Liszt were among those who accepted the challenge, while Beethoven upstaged them all by creating a masterpiece in the 33 Diabelli Variations Op. 120.

In August 1821, despite the disbandment of his orchestra, Schubert decided to turn once more to orchestral composition. The Seventh Symphony in E major never progressed beyond the sketch which still survives in the British Museum. In 1846 Schubert's brother Ferdinand invited Mendelssohn to complete it; Mendelssohn died before he could do so, and in 1868 *his* brother presented it to Sir George Grove who passed it on to the Royal College of Music in London. A full reconstruction of the score was completed by the Austrian composer and conductor Felix Weingartner in 1934.

Schubert seeks Beethoven's approval with the dedication of his Op. 10 Variations

Why did Schubert turn aside from his E major Symphony? It could well be that in the field of symphonic music he felt daunted by the achievement of Beethoven, for he did nothing to promote performances of his first six symphonies, almost denying their existence in a letter of January 1823 when he declared that '[I have] nothing for full orchestra which I could send out into the world with a clear conscience'.

There is a story of a visit by Schubert to Beethoven at about this time, which plays up the terror inspired in the young man by the great master. The story goes that Schubert, 'shy and speechless' and 'paralysed' with fear, went to present Beethoven with his 'Variations on a French Song'. Beethoven pointed out an error in the harmony, whereupon Schubert lost control of himself and fled from the house. There is no firm evidence that such a meeting took place, however. All we know for certain is that Schubert obtained Beethoven's permission for the Variations to bear a dedication to 'Herr Ludwig van Beethoven by his Worshipper and Admirer Franz Schubert' when they were published in April 1822. Beethoven must have been impressed with the work, for according to his nephew Karl he played it through 'almost daily' for several months.

There were other reasons for Schubert's abandonment of the E major Symphony. Once again he became embroiled with the theatre. In March 1821 he had applied unsuccessfully for the job of assistant conductor at the Kärntnertor Theatre, and he did work there briefly as a voice coach until bad time-keeping lost him that job too. Much more significant was the new opera he began working on in September, this time in collaboration with his friend Franz von Schober: towards the end of the year, Schubert moved back into Schober's house.

The composer's circle of friends was changing. In September the faithful Spaun left Vienna for Linz, where he remained for five years. Mayrhofer was becoming more and more reclusive, and Schubert began to socialise in smart drawing-rooms rather than cafés and bars. For three years, from 1820–22, he was a guest at the so-called 'Atzenbrugg Feast' held on the Atzenbrugg estate outside Vienna, where Schober's uncle was estate manager. There the guestlist included the painters Moritz von Schwind and Leopold Kupelweiser, and the dramatist Eduard von Bauernfeld. Apart from intellectual conversation, the house-party amused itself with charades, games and picnics. Kupelweiser depicted the leisured amusements of the company in two pictures, and Schubert published two volumes of Atzenbrugg dances.

Back in Vienna during the winter months the Atzenbrugg circle met two or three times a week for reading parties. They read from Goethe, Shakespeare, Homer, Ossian, Novalis and others. Whether or not there was a political dimension to these gatherings, they aroused the suspicion of the authorities and the participants felt obliged to adopt false names.

Such intellectual reading parties were very fashionable in German-speaking Europe, not least in the Prussian capital, Berlin. It was there in June 1821 that a very significant event occurred in the story of German opera with the wildly successful première of Weber's magic opera *Der Freischütz* (*The Freeshooter*). Attitudes began to change: even Vienna's powerful Italian impresario Domenico Barbaja began to see a future in German opera, commissioning Weber's *Euryanthe* in 1822. It was against this more encouraging background that Schober and Schubert set to work on a story invented by Schober with a little help

The painter Leopold Kupelwieser

Charades during a
Schubertiad
at Atzenbrugg

from Shakespeare. *Alfonso und Estrella* was to be a German grand opera, though the spirit of Rossini was still, as it were, looking over Schubert's shoulder.

The two young men worked on their opera while staying in the autumn of 1821 with a bishop related to Schober at his castle near the country town of St Pölten. It was an agreeable as well as productive time. 'In the evening,' Schubert told Spaun in a letter, 'we always compared notes on what we had done, then sent for beer, smoked our pipes and read.'

They returned to Vienna in time to attend the first performance in the Austrian capital of *Der Freischütz*, in a savagely cut version. This was not a success, but the opera fared better a few months later when, in February 1822, Weber himself came to Vienna to conduct two performances. Schubert and Schober introduced themselves to Weber and took him to an oratorio performance.

Their hopes for *Alfonso und Estrella* were doomed to disappointment. In the autumn of 1822 Schubert had to ask the Kärntnertor Theatre to return his manuscript. He sent it in vain to Weber in Dresden and the singer Anna Milder-Hauptmann in Berlin: the piece did not reach the stage until 1844 when it was given at Weimar in a version heavily edited by Liszt.

Schubert was so prolific that the ink-pot soon ran dry

The fact is that the opera in its original form seems to have pleased nobody. Vogl had warned Schubert that it would not be effective on the stage, and told Spaun that it was 'bad' and 'a perfect failure'. Naturally the fate of *Alfonso* caused Schubert deep disappointment, and indeed 1822 was a year of mixed fortunes for the composer. At least one of his old friends, Anton Holzapfel, felt that Schubert was no longer the cheerful companion he had once been. 'I rarely see him,' said Holzapfel in a letter of February 1822, 'and we don't hit it off very well, for his world is a very different one, as indeed it must be. His rather abrupt manner stands him in good stead, and will make a strong man and a mature artist of him.'

On the positive side, Schubert's solo songs and part songs were performed at concerts throughout 1822, and he continued to create new ones. In the years between 1821 and 1823, he continued his exploration of Goethe, setting four of the 200 or so love poems influenced by Persian poetry in Goethe's *West-Östlicher Divan*. 'Suleika 1' and 'Suleika 2' were in fact written by Marianne Jung, Goethe's thirty-year-old lover, who was thirty-six years younger than the poet. In 1821, Schubert set Goethe's 'Grenzen der Menschheit' ('Human Limitations') and two of Mignon's songs from *Wilhelm Meister*. In 1822 he set 'Wanderers Nachtlied' for the second time, the popular 'Der Musensohn' ('Son of the Muses'), 'An Die Entfernte' ('To the Distant Beloved'), 'Am Flusse' ('By the Stream') and 'Wilkommen und Abschied' ('Hail and Farewell').

Among the younger generation, Franz von Bruchmann contributed the poems of 'Am See' ('By the Lake') and 'Schwestergrüss' ('Sister's Greeting') among others. Words by Matthäus von Collin inspired three masterpieces: 'Wehmut' ('Melancholy'), 'Der Zwerg' ('The Dwarf') and 'Nacht und Träume' ('Night and Dreams'). The homosexual Count August von Platen provided Schubert with two heartbreaking poems – 'Die Liebe hat gelogen' ('Love Has Lied') and 'Du Liebst mich nicht' ('You Love Me Not'). Among the best of the settings of Friedrich Rückert are 'Du bist die Ruh' ('You Are Rest'), 'Lachen und Weinen' ('Laughter and Tears') and 'Dass sie hier gewesen' ('The Aura of her Presence'). And from Johann Senn, banished to his native Tyrol, Bruchmann brought back to Schubert in September 1822 two poems which became songs: 'Selige Welt' ('Blessed World') and 'Schwanengesang' ('Swansong').

In 1822 Schubert created a large-scale work for piano solo whose thematic treatment is based on his 1816 song 'Der Wanderer' to a poem by G. P. Schmidt of Lübeck. It was, as Schubert told Spaun in a letter, dedicated to 'a certain wealthy person', who happened to be a very able pianist – hence the technical difficulty of the piece. The Fantasy explores the Wanderer motif in various different ways, with a moving slow movement and a virtuosic fugue-like finale: it is regarded as the first large-scale 'monothematic' composition, the precursor of works on a similar pattern by later composers, among them César Franck. Franz Liszt, who was devoted to Schubert's music, made an arrangement in about 1851 of the *Wanderer Fantasy* for piano and orchestra. It seems clear that Schubert identified strongly with the Romantic stereotype of man on a lonely journey through life. Apart from the Fantasy and the song on which it was based, there's another 'Der Wanderer' song with words by Schlegel, as well as Seidl's 'Der Wanderer an den Mond', 'Das Wandern' (first song of the *Schöne Müllerin* cycle) and two settings of 'Wanderers Nachtlied'.

Let's hope Schubert was appropriately rewarded by that 'wealthy person' for his Fantasy. Disillusioned with his treatment in the theatre, Schubert decided in the later months of 1822 to dedicate his Mass No. 5 in A flat, which had occupied him on and off for three years, to the Emperor. He called the Mass 'Missa Solemnis' – whether in the knowledge that Beethoven had completed *his* mighty 'Missa Solemnis' in the

The powerful head of Franz Schubert in a cameo portrait

same year or not we don't know. In a December letter to Spaun, Schubert told him the work was shortly to be performed, but as was the case with *Alfonso* his hopes were disappointed. So was any hope he might have entertained of an official musical appointment, despite the flattering dedication. In 1824 Josef Eybler succeeded Salieri as court music director: Eybler considered performing a revised version of Schubert's 'Missa Solemnis' but abandoned the project on the grounds that it was too difficult and did not conform to the conventional expectations of a major church work. Schubert was not at his best in the fugal passages habitually demanded of liturgical composers at the time.

Schubert, a young man of twenty-five, desperately needed to enlarge his uncertain income, not least because of his association with the extravagant Schober, who had a weakness for Arabian carpets and Persian dressing-gowns, among other luxuries. It seems, according to one contemporary account, that '[Schober] made the fullest use of Schubert to extricate himself from financial embarrassments and to defray the expenditure which has already exhausted the greater part of his mother's fortune'.

Perhaps it was that kind of pressure that drove Schubert to sell the copyright of all his works published so far (they amounted to ten volumes) to Diabelli for a single payment of 800 florins, much to the distress of friends such as Sonnleitner and the Hüttenbrenners, who had helped to fund Schubert's first publications. Schubert then approached the publishers Sauer and Leidesdorf, and agreed to keep them supplied with songs over a two-year period for 480 florins a year. The young man may also have had some return from the use by the 'Hungarian Crown' inn of one of his songs for their mechanical musical clock.

Schubert omitted one important fact from his December letter to Spaun, namely that in October and November 1822 he had been working on his Eighth Symphony in B minor, the most beloved of the many works which Schubert was to leave unfinished. Great and glorious though Schubert's legacy to the world was, there's an element of truth in a phrase from the reminiscences of Anton Prokesch, who was a young army officer when Schubert met him at a reception in 1822. 'Great music slumbered in him,' wrote Prokesch, 'but it never came to such an awakening as he himself dreamed of and heard in his soul'. Of course, Prokesch could not have been remotely aware of the awakening Schubert *did* achieve. That awareness was reserved for future generations.

. V .

An Encounter With
the Erlking

The first time anyone had a chance to judge the merits of Schubert's 'Unfinished' Symphony was on 17 December 1865, when Johann Herbeck, who took a great interest in bringing Schubert's work to light, conducted the first ever performance in Vienna.

The question why this great work should have remained incomplete is one of music's most teasing riddles. Two movements of superlative quality were finished, and much of a third movement, a scherzo, exists in sketch form, so it does seem that Schubert set out to write a four-movement work. There have been various attempts to finish it, rounding out the sketch for the scherzo, and, in the case of Gerald Abraham in 1971, using the B minor entr'acte of the *Rosamunde* music as a finale. The theory that this may have been Schubert's intention is now discredited, for although the entr'acte is in the symphony's predominant key, it in no way matches the profound substance of the surviving first two movements. Nor does Schubert's sketch for the scherzo indicate that it would have worthily succeeded what had gone before. Schubert's biographer Alfred Einstein declared that 'nothing could ever have been fashioned from the material of this scherzo which could have

*The start of the
'Unfinished' Symphony*

approached the originality, power and skill of the two preceding movements'.

So did Schubert simply run out of appropriate ideas? Did he perhaps realise the stature of what he had already created and prefer to leave it rather than complete it in unworthy fashion? Or was he guided by his unfulfilled desire to write a 'grand' symphony which could challenge comparison with Beethoven? These two deeply moving, wistful essays did not perhaps seem suitable for public exhibition. It wasn't until Schubert turned, later, to the bold, extrovert key of C major in his Ninth Symphony that he achieved the 'grand' symphonic masterpiece he had longed for years to create, and Schubert promoted that for all he was worth. It seems the composer

Schubert with his Graz friends Anselm Hüttenbrenner and Johann Jenger

never tried to have the Eighth Symphony performed. Instead he gave it away.

On 10 April 1823, Schubert was appointed an honorary member of the Styrian Music Society in Graz, which was run by two of his close friends, Johann Jenger and Anselm Hüttenbrenner. The citation stated that 'although still young, [Schubert] has already proved by his compositions that he will one day rank high as a composer'. After a gap of some months, the reasons for which we shall explore in a moment, Schubert wrote to the society thanking them in effusive terms and promising to express his 'lively sense of gratitude' by presenting the society 'at the earliest opportunity with one of my symphonies in full score'.

It is unlikely that Schubert would have thought his two finished movements a suitable fulfilment of such a promise, but he did give the manuscript to Josef Hüttenbrenner to convey to his brother in Graz. An expression of gratitude, said Josef, for the honour the composer had received. It is uncertain whether Schubert intended the work to be passed on to the society or regarded as a private gift, a token of Schubert's sense of obligation to Anselm. Anyway, there was no doubt in Anselm's mind that he was entitled to keep the score, and he

*Schubert and Vogl in
action, with admiring
onlookers*

did so, making no attempt over the next thirty years to bring it to
public attention. He consigned it to a drawer in his house in Graz, and
there it lay until 20 April 1865 when Herbeck, tipped off by Josef
Hüttenbrenner, rescued it from a mass of other stored-away papers.
The story goes that Anselm would not let the manuscript out of his
sight until Herbeck has promised to conduct one of his own symphonies in Vienna. How mysterious and sad the story is – and we have
left out of the account so far its most tragic aspect.

In the summer of 1822, Schubert's relations with the singer
Michael Vogl deteriorated badly. Vogl had taken a poor view of *Alfonso
and Estrella*, and the absence of his backing no doubt had a good deal
to do with the rejection of the opera by the impresario Barbaja.

Whether for that reason or some other, Schubert treated Vogl in a discourteous manner quite at odds with his customary behaviour. Others of Schubert's friends complained that Schubert was acting in an offhand, superior fashion while indulging in a loose and extravagant life-style.

There are those who believe that Schubert was homosexual, and became involved in Vienna's homosexual underworld. As with so many other details of the composer's life, the true nature of his emotional attachments is unknown to us, but there is no firm evidence to confirm the homosexual theory. Certainly his male friendships were close, but the exchange of passionate protestations between friends was in keeping with the manners of the Romantic age. It is far more likely that, in the absence of marriage or a satisfactory love affair, Schubert was led by companions to experiment with female prostitutes.

The dramatist Eduard von Bauernfeld, whose reminiscences are an important source of information about Schubert, suggests that the composer led something of a double life, whose competing demands were not wholly resolved. He was, on the one hand,

Josef Kenner

> *amicable and modest, devoted to his friends from the bottom of his*
> *heart and acknowledging with affection the achievements of*
> *others . . . For what was evil and false he had a veritable hatred . . .*
> *[but] there were also times when a black-winged demon of sorrow and*
> *melancholy forced its way into Schubert's vicinity. Not altogether an*
> *evil spirit, it is true, since in the dark consecrated hours it often*
> *brought forth songs of the most agonising beauty. The conflict between*
> *unrestrained and boisterous living and the restless activity of spiritual*
> *creation is always exhausting if no balance exists in the soul.*
> *Fortunately in our friend's case, an idealised love was at work,*
> *mediating, reconciling, compensating.*

Another friend, Josef Kenner, was even more outspoken in his memoirs about the duality of Schubert's character. 'Anyone who knew

Schubert,' he recalled, 'knows that he had two natures foreign to each other, and how powerfully the craving for pleasure dragged his soul down to the slough of moral degradation.' Kenner blamed Schober outright for leading Schubert into dissipation.

Whatever the nature or extent of his sexual adventures, the result was that the young composer contracted syphilis and, in the autumn of 1822, he left Schober to take refuge in his father's house in the Rossau.

The primary stage of syphilis involves the appearance of an ulcerative sore, most usually on the genitalia; the secondary stage, which follows after weeks or months, can produce a widespread red rash and a raised temperature. The third stage, which is reached after a period of years, produces much more serious effects on the nervous system which can lead to what doctors call 'general paralysis of the insane' and other potentially lethal consequences. Schubert did not live long enough to experience the tertiary stage of the disease, though it may have been heralded by the general malaise, involving headaches, giddiness and nausea which afflicted him intermittently for the remaining six years of his life.

Schubert had good medical attention and received the best treatment available at the time, which would have consisted of the application or injection of mercury or arsenic, both poisonous substances in themselves with some of the side-effects associated with chemotherapy today, including loss of hair. Schubert was treated for the rash in Vienna's General Hospital for some weeks in the summer of 1823 (hence the delay in his response to the Graz society) and for a time wore a wig to conceal his temporary baldness. Feelings of shame meant that he was apt to conceal himself from his friends at this time.

The first documentary evidence we have of Schubert's illness is a letter of 28 February 1823 from the composer to court official Ignaz von Mosel. Schubert began the letter by apologising for not speaking to Mosel in person, saying that his health still prevented him from leaving the house. The use of the word 'still' confirms that he'd been ill for some time. But whatever physical discomfort he experienced, and however deep the associated depression, his creative impulse was not impaired; indeed it flourished and led him into hitherto unexplored territory.

The first onset of the disease coincided with the creation of the 'Unfinished' Symphony in October and November of 1822. Without wishing to draw too close a parallel between the events of Schubert's life and the products of his musical imagination, it does seem likely that the tragic quality of the music was at least to some extent related to the composer's own suffering, and the knowledge that his illness could lead to premature death: the passages in the major key seem to offer shafts of consoling light from another world. Interesting that years later Tchaikovsky should have chosen the key of B minor for his 'Pathétique' Symphony, that graphic account of personal despair.

Of course Schubert's 'Unfinished' is not overtly autobiographical, but if it did relate to his experience of what he regarded as a shameful illness, that fact would help to account for the near-secrecy which surrounded it. No mention of the work in progress to his friends, no attempt to have it performed. And no concluding movements after the first two. Perhaps after descending to the depths, a new and more hopeful mood possessed the composer, and for the moment he had nothing more to say in tragic vein.

The medical treatment cost money, and when Schubert wrote to Ignaz von Mosel in February 1823 his letter accompanied the score of the overture and third act of the rejected *Alfonso and Estrella*, in the hope no doubt that Mosel would use his influence at court to achieve a performance. In the same month Schubert complained to the publisher Diabelli that 'the appearance of two books of waltzes [on February 5] . . . was not carried out quite according to arrangements', suggesting that he hadn't been paid enough. On 24 February Diabelli published the *Wanderer Fantasy*, but in April Schubert decided to sever his connection with Diabelli altogether, accusing the firm, among other things, of undervaluing his songs. 'I am now in a position to obtain 200 florins per book,' he told them, requesting the return of all his manuscripts. His publishing hopes

A royalty statement for
Schubert, prepared by
Hüttenbrenner

now rested with the firm of Sauer and Leidesdorf, who proved to be
perpetually on the edge of bankruptcy and caused Schubert many
worries: nonetheless, 1823 proved a good year for him where publication was concerned, continuing the growth in public awareness
of his work which had begun with the appearance in March 1821 of
'Erlkönig', and had gradually gathered momentum as the months
went by.

Despite his illness and perhaps because of the isolation it forced upon him, Schubert was able to work hard: the first few months of 1823 were among the most productive of his life. In February he produced the Piano Sonata in A minor D784, a work which, like the 'Unfinished' Symphony, echoes the depression Schubert suffered at the time. In the words of pianist Mischa Donat, 'it is at once the bleakest and most anguished of his sonatas . . . the music [has] an extraordinary feeling of world-weariness'.

In quite a different vein was the light opera Schubert composed in March and April 1823, based on the *Lysistrata* of Aristophanes. Schubert managed to reflect in his music the light touch of his librettist I. F. Castelli. For all its merits, *Der Häusliche Krieg* was not seen until 1861, when Johann Herbeck conducted a concert performance – a performance attended by the aged Castelli who was greatly moved because his composer colleague had not survived to be there with him.

If this ironic comedy was perhaps the best of Schubert's operatic essays, *Fierabras* was, according to Alfred Einstein, the worst. The libretto was by Josef Kupelwieser, secretary to the Court Opera, an appointment which should have increased the likelihood of a performance at the Kärntnertor Theatre. Schubert worked hard at the piece, continuing to do so during his stay in hospital in June and July and completing it during the two months he spent on holiday in Steyr and Linz with Vogl (their friendship now repaired) between mid-July and mid-September.

In a letter of 14 August, Schubert described himself to Schober, who was by then pursuing a theatre career in Breslau, as 'fairly well', though he knew his health prospects were uncertain: 'I almost begin to doubt,' he added, 'whether I shall ever completely recover.' But the fresh air, the change of scene, and social evenings with friends did cheer Schubert up, and he enjoyed relaxing with the poetry and prose of Sir Walter Scott. Vogl was a great enthusiast for Scott's 'The Lady of the Lake' which was later to provide Schubert with the words of three beautiful songs, among them the beloved 'Ave Maria'.

The Kärntnertor Theatre in
Vienna

In early October, *Fierabras* — a romantic story set in the time of Charlemagne — was completed and handed over to the Kärntnertor Theatre, where everyone expected it to be produced without delay, reflecting a new-found enthusiasm for German opera. 'In addition to Weber's *Euryanthe* and Kreutzer's *Der Taucher*,' reported Vienna's *Theaterzeitung* (*Theatre News*), 'the Kärntnertor is shortly to present the first grand opera by the highly promising Schubert, the brilliant composer of "Erlkönig" — *Fierabras*.'

The performance of *Euryanthe* duly took place on 25 October. It was not a success. Schubert was there, and when he met Weber next day, he tactlessly told him he preferred *Der Freischütz*, thus putting an end to their friendship. Schubert realised that Weber's failure was not a good omen for his own work. 'Weber's *Euryanthe* turned out disastrously,' Schubert wrote to Schober, 'and its poor reception was in my opinion quite justified. These circumstances leave me scarcely any hope for my opera.' Schubert's forebodings were well-founded. If a German opera by a famous and popular composer had to be withdrawn after just two performances, then what hope was there for a

German opera by someone still trying to get a foothold in the theatre? *Fierabras* was consigned to storage along with so many other Schubert creations until, in 1897, Felix Mottl conducted a revised version at Karlsruhe.

Meanwhile, after struggling for so long with the stage with so little success, Schubert discovered in 1823 the art-form which was to prove his ideal medium for dramatic expression. The origin of the song-cycle, a sequence of individual songs which taken together tell a story, dates back to the early seventeenth century, and it appealed strongly to composers of the romantic period. Beethoven produced his sequence *An die Ferne Geliebte* in 1816, and Schubert had experimented with Schlegel's *Abendröte* (Sunsets), but it was not until he came across the poems of Wilhelm Müller (1794–1827) that he found the perfect song-cycle material.

Die Schöne Müllerin (*The Beautiful Mill-Girl*) started life as an intellectual party game played by Müller and his friends at gatherings in Berlin in 1816 and 1817. The group would agree on a theme, and then each of them would adopt a different character. Together they played out the story, with each person making up his part as he went along. Müller's contributions were so good that he was persuaded to arrange them into a cycle and publish them under the title 'Seventy-seven poems from the posthumous papers of a travelling horn player'.

It was this volume, so the story goes, that Schubert picked up one day in the office of a friend, Benedikt Randhartinger. Left on his own when Benedikt was summoned by his boss, Schubert became totally immersed in Müller's poems, to the extent that he left the office with the book in his pocket without waiting for his friend's return. Baffled by the disappearance of both Schubert and his book, Randhartinger called next day to seek an explanation and retrieve his property. Müller's verses had prompted in the composer an irresistible urge to create, and by way of compensation for his apparent rudeness, he presented Randhartinger with the first songs of *Die Schöne Müllerin*.

The story of the poetic sequence has its roots in German folklore.

A young miller falls in love with his employer's daughter. His love is returned until a dashing young huntsman appears on the scene and steals the maiden for himself. The rejected miller drowns himself in the mill stream.

Here was a simple tale with strong, powerful emotions. Discarding the poems which he felt were insufficiently serious, Schubert devised a sequence of twenty songs linked together by a semi-quaver figure which represents the mill stream, a figure which changes to fit the mood of each song, all of them masterly. Many of the world's leading singers have made *Die Schöne Müllerin* part of their repertoire, not least the great German baritone Dietrich Fischer-Dieskau. Recently, in his retirement as a singer, he appeared in the role of narrator on a recording of the cycle by Ian Bostridge and Graham Johnson, reading the poet's prologue and epilogue to the sequence.

Schubert started work on *Die Schöne Müllerin* in May 1823. It could well be that in the sad fate of the young man in the story Schubert found an echo of his own desolate feelings, expressed at the time in a poem he wrote on 8 May: 'Mein Gebet' ('My Prayer'):

See, my tortured existence lies shattered in the dust,
A prey to terrible affliction,
Nearing eternal destruction.

But whatever his inner feelings, he continued to work on the cycle during his stay in hospital and completed it in November. To Schober he was dismissive of what must be regarded as one of his greatest achievements. 'I have composed nothing since the opera,' wrote Schubert, 'except a few mill-songs.' It is good to report that unlike so many of Schubert's creations, the 'mill-songs' soon found their way to a wide public: they were all published in 1824 in five books.

No sooner had Schubert completed *Die Schöne Müllerin* than he turned yet again to the theatre, though once again his prospects of success were, to say the least, uncertain. The failure of Weber's *Euryanthe* had a lot to do with the libretto, by Helmine von Chézy, a poetess from Dresden, described by one of Schubert's friends as 'extremely good-natured, a little ridiculous and not particularly distinguished for her cleanliness'. Her literary skill left a lot to be desired as well, but Schubert apparently did not resist when Josef Kupelwieser invited Von Chézy to collaborate with the composer on a play with music called *Rosamunde, Princess of Cyprus*. The authoress later recalled that 'a beautiful girl whom Kupelwieser loved, Fraulein Neumann, an actress at the Theater an der Wien, was to have the play for her benefit'. The piece was staged on 20 December 1823, and the critics duly went to town in condemnation of the text, which they described as 'empty', 'tedious' and 'unnatural', though they were warm in praise of Schubert's contributions. 'The musical accompaniment by Schubert,' said the *Wiener Zeitschrift*, 'left no doubt as to this popular master's genius.' But Schubert was not able to save the play, which closed after only two performances. And Ms Treumann left Kupelwieser for an actor.

Two of the vocal pieces in the score, the delightful Shepherds' Chorus and the Huntsmen's Chorus, were so successful that they were published with reasonable speed. As for the rest of the numbers,

*Schubert's devoted friend
Moritz von Schwind*

several of which had their origin in earlier pieces, they lay gathering dust until the 1860s, when they were unearthed through the persistent researches of Sir George Grove. What we know as the very popular overture to *Rosamunde* is really nothing of the kind. It is rather the overture to Schubert's earlier opera *Die Zauberharfe* under another name. And this was not the music used before the curtain rose on the only two performances of *Rosamunde*: that was the overture to *Alfonso and Estrella*.

It is a relief to be able to state that *Rosamunde* marked the end of Schubert's sustained but ill-starred assault on the theatre. In future he would focus his attention on areas where he could be his own master: songs, instrumental music and the 'grand symphony' he was still longing to compose.

Underlying all his activity was a growing sadness, engendered not just by illness but by the break-up of his circle of friends. By the end of 1823 only two of his closest companions, the painter Moritz von Schwind and the philosopher Franz von Bruchmann, were still living in Vienna. The rest were dispersed elsewhere in search of jobs, inspiration, or just themselves. It soon became apparent that without the likes of Schober, Spaun and the artist Leopold Kupelwieser, who left for Italy towards the end of 1823, the reading parties and Schubertiads could not survive. A series of letters to absent friends chronicle developments in Schubert's state of health and the disintegration of his social life.

On the evening of 23 November 1823, Schubert was well enough to attend a farewell party for Kupelwieser on his departure for Rome. He was confined to his bed during the day, but Schwind, writing to Schober, was hopeful that he would soon be up and about. Schubert had sought out the best doctors in Vienna and followed their advice to the letter, and, reported Schwind, 'they already speak of a period of four weeks, after which he will probably be completely restored to health'.

In a letter to Schober on 24 December, Schwind repeated: 'Schubert is better and it will not be long before he has his own hair again, which had to be cut off because of the rash. He wears a very cosy wig.' On New Year's Eve, Schubert was well enough to go to a party at the house of the painter Ludwig Mohr, a new recruit to the circle who on 19 January 1824 hosted the first Schubertiad for two months. On 31 January, the composer was fit enough to celebrate his birthday at The Crown.

In February 1824, Schober received even better news from Schwind:

Franz von Bruchmann

> *Schubert is keeping a fourteen-day fast and is confined to his house.*
> *He looks much better and is very cheerful, very comically hungry, and*
> *is writing innumerable quartets, German dances and variations. He*
> *has given up his wig and reveals a pretty head of short curly hair.*

A few days later Schwind was writing again: 'Schubert is now quite well. He says that after a few days of the new treatment he could feel his complaint lose its grip and everything was different.'

But if Schubert's physical health was improving, his state of mind was still depressed, partly no doubt because the people he met at social gatherings had become less congenial. 'The readings are beginning to be somewhat different,' Schwind told Schober in November 1823. 'The crowd and the mixture of guests is irksome and I do not feel at home.'

A letter from Schubert suggested that Schober's absence was partly to blame:

> *Our circle, as indeed I expected, has lost its central focus without*
> *you . . . what is the good of a lot of quite ordinary students and*
> *officials to me? If Bruchmann is not there, we go on for hours hearing*
> *nothing but eternal talk about riding, fencing, horses and hounds.*

Schwind echoed Schubert's sentiments when writing yet again to Schober in December 1823:

> *I am on the point of resigning from the readings, for the reading is so*
> *stifled by business affairs and pranks that even to gather together*

A picture showing Schubert's curly hair — or was it his 'cosy wig'?

undisturbed is impossible. If you or Senn suddenly appeared in our midst we should be truly ashamed of such company.

The reading circle's days were clearly numbered.

Schubert signalled the end of the line in a letter to Kupelwieser on 31 March 1824: 'Our society has done itself to death owing to a reinforcement of that rough chorus of beer-drinkers and sausage-eaters; its dissolution is due in a couple of days.'

Anton von Doblhoff wrote to Schober on 2 April 1824: 'Yesterday our reading circle was formally suspended. Oh, where are those serene and happy times? Schubertiads are hardly mentioned any more: Schubert himself cannot sing, and Vogl will sing only in agreeable and respectable society.'

A diary kept by Schubert for a short time in March 1824 reveals a sense of despairing isolation: 'There is no one who understands the joy and pain of others. We always believe that we are coming together, and always we move only side to side. What torture it is for those who recognise this.'

On 31 March he gave vent to his feelings in a heart-rending letter to Kupelwieser in Rome:

I feel myself to be the most unhappy wretched creature in the world. Imagine a man whose health will never be right again and who, in his despair over this, constantly makes things worse instead of better; imagine a man, I say, whose brightest hopes have come to nothing, to whom the happiness of love and friendship offer nothing but pain, whose enthusiasm (at least the stimulating kind) for beauty threatens to vanish; and then ask yourself if he is not indeed a wretched unhappy creature.

Quoting from *Gretchen am Spinnrade* Schubert continued:

'My peace is gone, my heart is heavy, I shall find it never and nevermore.' Thus indeed I can now sing every day, for every night when I go to sleep, I hope I will not wake again, and each morning reminds

The glamour of Vienna's waltzing era re-created on stage.

Ludwig van Beethoven (1770–1827), another artist who influenced Schubert greatly.

A painting by Leopold Kupelwieser of Schubert and friends on excursion to Atzenbrugg.

The famous watercolour portrait of Schubert by Wilhelm August Rieder, 1825.

A group of Schubert's friends, gathered at one of the renowned Schubertiads.

Robert Schumann (1810–1856), one of Schubert's first champions, in a portrait by Hans Best. It was Schumann who unearthed much of the composer's work, including the 'Great' C major Symphony.

George Grove, in a cartoon by Spy *for* Vanity Fair *in 1891. Grove was another of Schubert's posthumous supporters, and was responsible for tracking down many of the early symphonies as well as the music for* Rosamunde.

August Manns, in another Spy cartoon. Manns was the German-born conductor of the Crystal Palace concerts which saw the first performances of much of Schubert's work, including the 'Unfinished' Symphony.

me only of yesterday's unhappiness. Thus, joyless and friendless, I
should pass my days, if Schwind did not visit me occasionally and
bring me a breath of those sweet days that are past.

But Schubert was at least struggling to make a positive response to his
suffering. 'Pain sharpens the understanding and strengthens the mind,'
he told himself in his diary. Certainly suffering did nothing to impede
the flow of creative ideas. 'So far as songs are concerned,' he told
Kupelwieser, 'I have not done much that is new, but I have tried my
hand at several instrumental things, for I wrote two quartets for violins, viola and cello and an octet, and I intend to write another quartet
and generally to pave my way to [the] grand symphony in this way.'

Schubert composed his Octet in F for strings and woodwind in
February 1824, to a commission from Count Troyer who asked for a
work 'exactly like Beethoven's Septet'. Apart from adding an extra
instrument, Schubert did as he was told, producing a piece with the
same type and number of movements and the same key structure as
Beethoven's.

The first of the two quartets mentioned in the letter to Kupelwieser is No. 13 in A minor. Composed in February and March 1824,
it was dedicated to Ignaz Schuppanzigh, Vienna's most famous violinist and leader of the Schuppanzigh Quartet. They gave the first
performance on 14 March, an occasion described by Schwind in a
letter to Schober: 'Schubert's quartet was performed, rather slowly
in his opinion, but in such a way that the tune stays in one's head, as
with the songs.' The slow movement quotes the Andantino in
Rosamunde, and the Minuet (which got much applause, according to
Schwind) quotes from Schubert's song 'Die Götter Griechenlands'
('The Gods of Greece'), the words of which are very much in keeping with Schubert's feelings at this time:

> *Beauteous world, where art thou?*
> *Return again, fair springtime of nature;*
> *Ah, your fabled dream lives only in the enchanted realm of song.*

The A-minor quartet fared much better than many of Schubert's compositions, for not only was it performed soon after it was finished, but published too.

As soon as he had completed the A-minor quartet, Schubert set to work on what was to be his greatest work in the medium, the quartet No. 14 in D minor, known by the name of the song which provided the theme of the slow movement, 'Death and the Maiden'. There's no record of a performance of this magnificent work in Schubert's lifetime, and it had to wait until three years after his death for publication.

While working on this instrumental masterpiece in March, Schubert did produce four songs, all of them settings of poems by Mayrhofer. The two men had grown apart, owing to 'changed views of life' according to the poet, so maybe the songs were an attempt to heal the breach. 'Abendstern' broods on the plight of the evening star which 'sows no seeds, sees no fruit and bears its grief alone'; 'Auflösung' ('Dissolution') uses the setting sun as a symbol of the transitory nature of life; 'Der Sieg' ('Victory') expresses a longing for 'the unclouded life, so pure and deep and clear'. The fourth of these Mayrhofer songs is 'Gondelfahrer' ('Gondolier').

Whatever differences there may have been between Mayrhofer and Schubert, it seems that they still shared a gloomy view of life, but there's no trace of this in other products of the early months of 1824, among them cheerful choruses, vocal quartets, piano duets, dances and the Introduction, Theme and Variations for flute and piano, written for the brilliant flautist, Ferdinand Bogner. Why Schubert should have chosen as the theme for this unashamed exercise in virtuoso display one of the most moving of the *Schöne Müllerin* songs, 'Trockne Blumen' ('Withered Flowers') remains a mystery.

In the spring and early summer of 1824, Schubert's health was variable, but on 7 May he was well enough to attend the first performance of Beethoven's Ninth Symphony, together with parts of the Missa Solemnis. Later that month, on 28 May he left Vienna to spend a second summer with the Esterházy family at their summer residence of Zseliz.

Significantly he left behind the script of a dramatic fairy-tale called *Der Kurze Mantel* (*The Short Cloak*) for which he'd been asked to write the music; even though brother Ferdinand sent it on to him, Schubert continued to ignore it. The theatre had lost its appeal for him.

The summer in Zseliz did him good: on 21 September he wrote to Schober that he'd been in good health for five months. He also enjoyed a high standard of living. Whereas before he'd lived in the servants' quarters, the Esterházys now treated him as a guest, with his own room in the castle, a seat at the family dinner-table and a proper salary for a well-known composer: 100 florins a month.

The job, too, was more rewarding if only because the young countesses were now accomplished musicians: Marie, now twenty-one, was an excellent pianist and Karoline at eighteen was a promising singer as well as a pianist. For them Schubert wrote two piano duet masterpieces, the 'Grand Duo' and the 'Variations on an Original Theme', and when the Esterházys' baritone friend Baron von Schönstein came to visit, the party sang vocal quartets in the evening, including the first performance of one of Schubert's finest part-songs, 'Gebet' ('Prayer').

Karoline Esterházy

In the course of the summer Schubert fell in love with Karoline, rather in the manner of an adoring, humble medieval troubadour. Schubert told Schober in August about the 'attractions of a certain star', implying that he knew Countess Karoline was beyond his reach.

Although Zseliz offered many attractions and distractions, and the composer was able to report to his brother that he was 'better able to find happiness and peace in myself', Schubert hankered after what was missing. On 21 September he wrote to Schober:

> *If only we were together, you Schwind, Kuppel [Kupelwieser] and I, any misfortune would seem but a trivial matter; but here we are, separated, each in a different corner and that is what makes me unhappy. I want to exclaim with Goethe 'Who will bring back an hour of that sweet time?' . . . Now I sit here alone in the depths of the Hungarian country, whither I unfortunately let myself be enticed a second time, without having a single person to whom I could speak a sensible word.*

In a poem called 'Complaint to the People', Schubert attributed his spiritual malaise to the prevailing state of society:

> *These idle times which hinder the fulfilment of all greatness destroy me too. Even golden verse is foolishly mocked by the people, no longer attentive to its powerful message. Only by the gift of sacred art can we still image forth the strength and achievements of former times, allay the pain which can never be reconciled with fate.*

An immediately tangible effect of the triviality which Schubert deplored was the failure of his publishers to do him justice. 'With Leidesdorf,' he complained to Schober, 'things have gone badly so far: he cannot pay, nor does a single soul buy anything, either my things or any others, except wretched fashionable stuff.'

After such a diatribe from a man who considered himself at odds with the times, it is curious to come across the following review of some of Schubert's vocal pieces:

The composer of these songs proves himself a respectable talent which, with the fresh courage of youth, disdains the old well trodden ways and clears a new path . . . but the reviewer deems himself entitled to speak . . . about the unwarrantably strong inclination to modulate again and again, with neither rest nor respite, which is a veritable disease of our time and threatens to grow into a modulation-mania to which unfortunately even famous composers succumb either willingly or for the sake of following the fashion.

On 17 October, a month earlier than planned, Schubert returned to Vienna and to his father's house, where he was to remain until spring 1825.

At last we once again get a glimpse of Schubert in a more buoyant state of mind. As Schwind wrote to Schober on 8 November 1824: 'Schubert is here, well and divinely frivolous, rejuvenated by delight and pain and a pleasant life.'

. VI .

Hopes Renewed

On his return from Upper Austria, Schubert moved back into his father's house, where he lived a quiet life for a few months and composed only a few minor pieces; there's no record of socialising until Christmas 1824, which he spent with the friend who was closest to him at the time, Moritz von Schwind, at his family home, fancifully named 'Moonshine House'. Schwind, whose devotion to Schubert remained undimmed till his death in 1871, decorated the Christmas tree with his own drawings and quotations from Schubert's songs. On Christmas Eve there was a party with a crowd of friends.

On 29 January 1825 the first in a weekly series of Schubertiads was held at the house of Josef Witteczek, son-in-law of Professor Watteroth, dedicatee of Schubert's *Prometheus* in 1816, but Schubert, was not there. For him, 1825 began when he moved from his father's home to take rooms next door to 'Moonshine House'. Schwind duly reported the move to Schober: 'Schubert is well and busy again after a certain period of idleness. He has recently come to live next door to us, where the ale-house is, on the second floor in a very pretty room.' Schober was also told that the new series of Schubertiads was continuing, with Vogl singing, though the composer was not often present.

Eduard von Bauernfeld

It was in February 1825 that Schwind introduced Schubert to a new friend, the dramatist and amateur musician Eduard von Bauernfeld, and the two men hit it off straightaway as drinking companions and piano duet partners. But the acquisition of a new friend was counterbalanced with quarrels among old ones.

The loyalties of the Schubertians were divided by a dispute between Bruchmann and Schober, who came to blows over Schober's secret love affair with Bruchmann's sister Justina. While Schober could be a good friend, he was a notorious womaniser, and Bruchmann was understandably anxious for his sister's welfare and reputation, the more so because the affair was kept secret from their parents, a sign perhaps that Schober's intentions were not entirely honourable. In March 1825, Bruchmann forced the affair into the open with the result that (as Kupelwieser's fiancée reported to him in a letter to Naples) 'Schubert and Schwind are in open feud with Bruchmann. They both seem to me like children and indeed they give vent to their hatred childishly. They do not meet any more at all and behave like great enemies.'

Schubert and Schwind were obviously at one in siding with Schober in this matter: indeed they were close in their routine of life. 'We meet daily,' said Schwind early in 1825, 'and, as far as I can, I share his whole life with him . . . I always visit Schubert early in the morning and for the rest of the day each sees how best to use it.' But soon there was a rift in this friendship too. It seems that Schubert had been offended by a member of the family of Schwind's girlfriend Anna Hönig. Without telling Schwind the reason, he repeatedly refused invitations to the Hönigs' house, causing Schwind to suspect that he himself had offended Schubert in some way. Schwind wrote a series of puzzled, mildly reproachful letters to the composer, who showed some impatience with the whole business:

Schwind is a regular tool-player and wool-teaser, for I do not know which of the letters he wrote me is the more confused. Never has such a rigmarole of sense and nonsense come my way. Unless he has done some very fine things these days, such brainless chatter is not to be forgiven.

However sublime Schubert's inner vision could be, his everyday existence was beset by such apparently trivial quarrels and reconciliations. Whatever the rights and wrongs of his tiff with Schwind, it had all been forgotten by the time Schubert returned from his extended holiday in the summer of 1825.

In those early months of 1825 there's some evidence that Schubert became emotionally attached to a girl whose identity is not clear. 'I am still in love with Clotilde,' confessed Bauernfeld at this time, 'as Moritz is with his Nettel. Schubert sniggers at us both, but is not quite heart-whole himself.' Could the person in question have been the beautiful and talented actress Sophie Müller, who lived an hour's drive from Vienna in Hietzing? Schubert visited Sophie five times in a few weeks for music and conversation. But Vogl was with him on these visits, and after Vogl left for Steyr in early April, Schubert visited Sophie less often – so the trail grows cold.

During April and May 1825, Schubert completed one and started another piano sonata. The unfinished Sonata in C major, posthumously published under the title 'Relique' ('Relic'), breaks off in the middle of the third movement, but is a masterpiece all the same. The complete A minor Sonata D845 is one of Schubert's greatest piano works and something of a landmark in his musical development. Free and melodic, yet solidly constructed, it shows that Schubert had learned to adapt the traditional classical form of the sonata to his own more romantic needs. When it was published early in 1826, the A minor sonata was warmly received by the critics, who noted Schubert's new approach to form. Leipzig's *Allgemeine Musicalische Zeitung* commented, 'It moves so freely and originally within its confines, and sometimes so boldly and curiously, that it might not unjustly have been called a Fantasy.'

The sonata's opening theme with its threatening insistent tread, can also be heard in Schubert's song 'Totengräbers Heimweh'

Sophie Müller: a sweetheart of Schubert's?

*Steyr, where Schubert took
a number of holidays over
the years*

('Gravedigger's Longing') composed in April 1825. In the piano part, the theme accompanies the words:

Abandoned by all,
Cousin only to Death,
I wait at the brink,
Staring longingly into the grave.

However, on about 20 May 1825, Schubert was able to put such extremely gloomy sentiments out of his mind, setting off to join Michael Vogl on a musical tour of Upper Austria which was to last five months.

Schubert took with him his nearly completed cycle of songs from Sir Walter Scott's *The Lady of the Lake*. Scott was enormously popular throughout Europe at this time, and on their tour Schubert and Vogl performed the songs wherever they went, with such success that Schubert dared to hope they would bring him international fame. On 25 July he wrote home:

I intend to follow a different procedure with the publication of these
songs, since they bear the celebrated name of Scott at their head, and
so might arouse more curiosity, and with the addition of the English
text, might also make me better known in England.

There are five songs altogether, the most famous of them being 'Ellen's Prayer', better known as the 'Ave Maria' which was as popular in Schubert's time as it is today.

Schubert was delighted to find that his fame was widespread in Upper Austria: 'I find my compositions everywhere,' he reported. And it wasn't just the printed music that was in demand, for Vogl and he were a formidable performing team. 'The manner in which Vogl sings and I accompany, in which we seem to be one,' Schubert told his brother, 'is something quite new and extraordinary to these people.'

After a fortnight in Steyr, Schubert and Vogl went to the popular resort of Gmunden on beautiful Lake Traun, where Schubert was able to finish *The Lady of the Lake* songs and start work on a new symphony. They stayed in Gmunden for six weeks in the house of Ferdinand Traweger, a wealthy music-loving merchant. Three miles along the lakeside was Ebenzweier Castle, the scene of many a musical gathering.

On 15 July they set off for Linz, arriving too late to meet up with their old friend Josef Spaun, who'd lived in the town since leaving Vienna in 1821 but who'd just started a new job in Lemberg. So Schubert's host was Spaun's bother-in-law Anton Ottenwalt, whose letters leave no doubt that Schubert was well in body and mind:

> 'Schubert looks so well and strong,' Ottenwalt wrote to Spaun, '[and he] was so friendly and communicative . . . we sat together until not far from midnight, and I have never seen him like this, nor heard: serious, profound and as though inspired. How he talked of art, of poetry, for his youth, of friends and other people who matter, for the relationship of ideals to life, etc! I was more and more amazed at such a mind.'

Schubert's own letter of 21 July to Spaun confirms the impression conveyed by Ottenwalt. He said he was 'perfectly happy', and although he was genuinely sorry to have missed his old friend, he expressed his feelings in light-hearted fashion:

*Schubert's brother
Ferdinand*

*Here I sit at Linz half dead with sweating in this frightful heat and
you are not here! Aren't you ashamed? Linz without you is like a body
without soul, like a headless horseman, or like a soup without salt. If
Jägermayr did not keep such good beer, and they had not a passable
wine on the Castle Hill, I should have to hang myself on the
promenade with the legend: 'From sorrow over the departed soul at
Linz.'*

There was plenty to distract the composer from such unhappy
ideas. Five miles outside Linz was Steyrigg Castle, the home of
Count and Countess Weissenwolf, where Schubert and Vogl spent
many an evening eating, drinking and music-making. Schubert dedicated his *Lady of the Lake* songs to Countess Sophie, who'd long
admired Schubert's music, never more so than when she heard
these songs. Schubertiads were also held at the nearby monastery of
St Florian.

On 25 July Schubert and Vogl returned to Steyr. From there
Schubert wrote home assuring the family of his continued good
health. Having been through the valley of the shadow himself, he
took a rather brisk line with his ailing brother Ferdinand:

*He has doubtless been ill seventy-seven times again and has thought
eight times that he was going to die, as though dying were the worst
that can happen to a man! If only he could once see these heavenly
mountains and lakes, the sight of which threatens to crush or engulf
us, he would not be so attached to puny human life, nor regard it as
otherwise than good fortune to be confided to earth's indescribable
power of creating new life.*

In mid-August, Vogl and Schubert embarked on a three-day journey
to the mountain town of Bad Gastein, famous since Roman times for
its healing waters, snowcapped mountains and waterfalls. On the
way they passed through the Salzburg countryside which Schubert
described for the benefit of housebound Ferdinand:

Think of a garden several miles in extent, with countless castles and estates in it peeping through the trees; think of a river winding through it in manifold twists and turns; think of meadows and fields like so many carpets of the finest colours, then of the many roads tied round them like ribbons; and lastly avenues of enormous trees to walk in for hours, all enclosed by ranges of the highest mountains as far as the eye can reach, as though they were guardians of this glorious valley; think of all this and you will have a faint conception of its inexpressible beauty.

It is clear from this, and Schubert's many other declarations of love for the countryside, that for him the fields and the sky, the flowers and the mountains, offered not just an aesthetic experience but a spiritual one too. During his stay at Gastein, Schubert was overjoyed to meet an old acquaintance who saw nature in a similar light. He was Johann Ladislaus Pyrker, poet, playwright and, since 1820, Patriarch of Venice. Pyrker belonged to a breed of liberal churchmen who felt the presence of God not just in a church but all around them. Schubert was moved to set one of Pyrker's poems, 'Die Allmacht' ('Omnipotence'), a hymn of praise to God as revealed in nature:

Great is Jehovah;
Heaven and earth proclaim His might.
You hear it in the raging storm
And in the rushing of forest streams,
And in the murmuring of forest trees;
You see it in the waving golden corn;
In the glowing splendour of sweet flowers,
In the brightness of a starry sky . . .

Other poets Schubert set to music between 1825 and 1828, apart from the great names – Shakespeare, Scott and Goethe – included Wilhelm Müller, author of *Die Schöne Müllerin*, Karl Wilhelm Schlegel, and his brother August Wilhelm. There was also businessman and amateur poet Jakob Craigher whom Schubert met early in 1825. He was a good linguist and useful translator, and provided among other things the poem for Schubert's 'Die Junge Nonne'. Johann Gabriel Seidl was a government official and fashionable journalist: Schubert set eleven of his poems, including 'Der Wanderer an den Mond' ('The Wanderer on the Moon'). Franz von Schlechta, an aristocrat and former school-friend of Schubert, provided the composer with the texts of six songs including the well-known 'Fischerweise'. Other poets were the Graz poet and teacher Karl Gottfried von Leitner and a writer from Leipzig, Johann Friedrich Rochlitz. Schubert did not necessarily require great words to create a great song.

While Schubert was in Gastein, he set another Pyrker poem to music, 'Das Heimweh' ('Homesickness'), created a piano sonata in D major and continued with the symphony he'd begun in Gmunden.

The identity of this symphony is uncertain and much-debated. Traditionally it has been referred to as the 'Gastein' Symphony and presumed lost or missing, but recent writers, among them John Reed in his biography the 'Master Musicians' series (1987), have advanced the theory that the 'Gastein' Symphony was in fact the first sketch of the 'Great' C major Symphony, D944. There are no hard and fast facts to support either view, but the new one makes sense of Schubert's declared intention of 31 March 1824 to 'pave my way to a grand symphony': the 'Great' C major is unquestionably grand. If this theory is correct, then between March 1824 and March 1828 Schubert's last symphony grew from an idea to a sketch to a finished masterpiece.

The 'Great' C major is the exact opposite of the 'Unfinished' Symphony. The 'Unfinished' is in a minor key, intensely personal and poignant in feeling. The 'Great', on the other hand, is in an uncompromisingly major key, and carefully constructed in a conventional sequence of movements. It's often said that the 'Unfinished' represents the private composer, pouring out his soul for anyone who cares to listen, in the manner of a Hamlet soliloquy, while the 'Great' represents the public composer seeking to address and inspire the multitude. Seen in another perspective, the two works exemplify the difference between the depressed, introverted and sick Schubert of 1822 and the happy, sociable and relatively healthy Schubert of 1825.

On 4 September, Schubert and Vogl returned in a roundabout way to Gmunden, arriving there about 10 September. On the 17th they went back to Steyr for a fortnight before returning to Linz around 1 October for farewell parties at the Ottenwalt's and the Weissenwolf's. Then Schubert and Vogl went their separate ways, Vogl to Italy, Schubert home to Vienna.

That Schubert's friends missed him enormously is clear from their letters, which are full of excited anticipation of a grand reunion of the Schubert circle. Schwind wrote on 14 August to say how much he was looking forward to the first Schubertiad, and at Steyr Schubert received a letter from Bauernfeld asking if he'd like to take lodgings with himself and Schwind. Schubert replied that although such a plan would suit him very well, he wasn't prepared to commit himself to an indefinite proposal. 'However,' he continued, 'should anything suitable turn up, I shall find means of parting from my landlord in a decent manner.' He was right to be cautious, for the plan came to nothing. Schubert returned to his old lodgings next door to Schwind, remaining there till Autumn 1826.

Also in his reply to Bauernfeld, Schubert said how much he was looking forward to seeing Schober and Kupelwieser again. They had both returned to Vienna in his absence, Schober in July, Kupelwieser in the first week of October. So for all concerned there was ample cause for celebration when Schubert came home in early October. 'Schubert is back,' reported Bauernfeld. 'Inn and coffee house gatherings with friends, often till two or three in the morning.' Bauernfeld even composed an ode to indulgence:

> *Shamefully we confess*
> *Every night*
> *Drinking and laziness*
> *Giving us delight.*

But the Schubert circle was changing, both in personnel and the nature of its gatherings. Kupelwieser began to spend more time with his beloved fiancée Johanna, while Bauernfeld joined Schwind, Schober and Schubert at the core of the group. And whereas before they'd entertained themselves with music, readings and intellectual discussion, they now indulged in an endless round of parties, with the result that in the first three months after his return to Vienna, Schubert got very little work done. All he managed to fit in around his hectic social engagements were a few songs and piano duets, though it's possible he was also working on his symphony.

Gratified by the success of his *Lady of the Lake* songs, Schubert was full of hopes for the future. In his absence the Vienna Philharmonic Society had elected him a deputy member of the Council of Representatives, and now he found himself in the enviable position of having two publishers competing for his compositions.

Before he'd left for Upper Austria, Schubert had offered the as yet unfinished *Lady of the Lake* songs to the publishing house of Anton Pennauer. The manager of the company was keen enough on the project to write to the composer in Steyr, asking for a progress report. Then along came Matthias Artaria, offering 200 florins for the songs, much more than he'd been promised by Pennauer, and it was Artaria who published the songs in April 1826 with English as well as German texts.

For some months now, as indicated in his letter home of 25 July 1825, Schubert had been convinced that bilingual editions of his songs would bring him success abroad, and one of the first things he did on his return to Vienna was to pay a visit to Jakob Craigher to seek his help as a translator. Craigher assisted with bilingual editions of up to seven songs, but they did nothing to advance Schubert's reputation outside Austria.

However, in the Austrian capital, his work was much in demand, sought after not only by the distinguished Artaria who had published Mozart, Haydn and Beethoven, but by three other publishing houses, Sauer and Leidesdorf, Pennauer, and T. Weigl, with the Diabelli firm still continuing to bring out the works it had acquired before Schubert left the company in 1823. One publishing firm, Cappi and Co., an offshoot of Diabelli, thought it worthwhile to issue an engraving of an 'extremely good likeness of the composer Franz Schubert painted by Rieder'. The Berlin *Allgemeine Musicalische Zeitung* was on the wrong track when it reported that although Schubert's 'first-fruits, especially the *Erl King*, found a public', that public 'seems to be diminishing'.

Publications of Schubert's songs doubled between 1825 and 1826 and again between 1827 and 1828, while his name appeared more and more frequently in concert programmes, especially those of the Philharmonic Society, which on 14 March decided to commission the first biography of the composer.

Although in his earlier years Schubert expressed disgust with the frivolous tastes of the Viennese, coupled with the name of Rossini, he was now happy enough to respond to the demand for showy pieces to please the public. Publishers often added colourful titles, many in French, to these pieces to increase their popular appeal. The Rondo in B minor for violin and piano D895 was marketed as 'Rondeau Brillant', the three-movement piano duet work based on a Hungarian melody was put on sale by Artaria in April 1826 as 'Divertissement à la Hongroise', and the rather later sonata movement in A minor for four hands came out in May 1828 under the inappropriate title 'Lebensstürme' ('Life's Storms'). Schubert's crowd-pleasing efforts often pleased the critics too. A writer in the Leipzig musical news declared that of all Schubert's works, the Variations on a theme from Hérold's opera *Maria*, was the most successful so far, indeed it 'must be numbered among the best of recent times'.

The year 1826 started off with a grand New Year's party which Schubert was not well enough to attend. But this was only a passing illness and a few days later Schubert was back on the party circuit: on 10 January he went to a Schubertiad at Schober's; he was there again on the 14th for a 'sausage ball', a party at which little Vienna sausages were served by the women to the men. On 25 January he went to Sophie Müller's for supper and music.

Schubert in the countryside, which for him was often a spiritual experience

All this high living meant that, despite the income he was receiving from publishers, he didn't get any richer. When Josef von Spaun returned to Vienna in April 1826 to take charge of the Public Lottery Office he expressed the situation thus: 'Back in Vienna again from Lemberg, I found Schubert in the full flowering of his talent. At last he was getting more recognition and receiving payment for his works, even though this was miserable in comparison with their worth. His position had improved, though it still continued to be unsatisfactory.'

Though he disliked the idea of a steady job, Schubert applied on 7 April for the post of vice-musical director at the Imperial Court chapel: the successful candidate was Josef Weigl. A little later Vogl persuaded Schubert to apply for a job as assistant conductor at the Kärntnertor Theatre. But the composer wrecked his chances by arguing at his audition with the leading soprano. She wanted to make changes in the score, Schubert refused, she kicked up a fuss and Schubert stormed out of the opera house. The sensible Spaun as usual got it right when he stated that Schubert had no desire to be a conductor anyway.

You'd have thought that with all the disappointment he'd endured Schubert would by this time have steered clear of the theatre in any shape or form. But no: he was encouraged by a change of management at the Kärntnertor Theatre to ask Bauernfeld to write a libretto for him. Schubert suggested an utterly unsuitable tale called *The Enchanted Rose*, a banal saga of knights, fairies, marches and processions with few dramatic possibilities. Bauernfeld's counter-proposal sounds hardly more promising. But *The Count of Gleichen*, he claimed, was better with its 'dramatic and musical contrasts, orient and occident, janissaries and knighthood, romantic wooing and wedded love, etc.'

Bauernfeld worked on the piece through the summer, which he spent on holiday in Carinthia and Upper Austria with Ferdinand von Mayrhofer. There were plans for Schwind, Spaun and Schubert to go to Linz in June, and Schubert hoped he could arrange a meeting with Bauernfeld to discuss progress either there or at Gmunden. But those plans came to nothing. On 10 July he wrote to Bauernfeld: 'I cannot possibly get to Gmunden or anywhere else, for I have no money at all, and altogether things go very badly with me.' Schubert spent some time at Schober's summer residence at Währing, not far from Vienna, where he felt 'dull and miserable' and impatient for Bauernfeld's libretto.

Towards the end of July, Bauernfeld returned to Vienna via the Danube, landing at Nussdorf to be greeted by Schwind and Schubert running out of a coffee-house to welcome him back. Bauernfeld described the happy scene in his diary: 'Great rejoicing! "Where is the opera?" asked Schubert. "Here!" and I solemnly handed him *The Count of Gleichen*.'

When Schubert sat down to read through the libretto his heart sank, for Bauernfeld's 'wedded love' turned out to be a bigamous marriage, involving the Count, The Countess Ottilie and a Saracen princess called Suleika. Schubert had little doubt that an opera which dealt with bigamy, except to stress what a terrible sin it was, would be blacklisted by the Viennese censors: and Bauernfeld's libretto was actually sympathetic towards the bigamous Count. Schubert told Bauernfeld of his concern, and in October their fears came true: the opera was banned. However, Schubert still wanted to compose the piece. Ten months later Bauernfeld reported that Schubert was working on the opera and there was some possibility of a production in Berlin. But *The Count of Gleichen* turned out to be yet another theatrical damp squib: Schubert got no further than eighty-eight pages of sketches.

Although Schubert may have felt bored during the summer at Währing, he did not spend all his time just waiting for Bauernfeld's libretto to arrive. He composed his last and arguably his greatest string quartet, No. 15 in G major. Full of driving rhythms, powerful unisons, foreboding tremolos and harmonic unrest, it was very probably influenced by Beethoven, whose quartet in B Flat Op. 130 had been premièred on 21 March. Also created that summer were Schubert's three Shakespeare songs: 'An Sylvia' ('Who is Sylvia?'), 'Ständchen' ('Hark, Hark the Lark') and 'Trinklied' ('Come, Thou

Monarch of the Vine'). The story goes that Schubert dreamed up 'Hark, Hark the Lark' in a beer garden and jotted it down on the back of the menu.

Renewed hopes of international fame arose when Schubert received a flattering invitation from the Swiss publisher H. G. Nägeli, to contribute to a collection of keyboard compositions with the grand title *Portal of Honour*. Schubert accepted the commission, asking for a high fee of 120 florins in advance. This was altogether too much for Nägeli, who terminated the negotiations there and then.

But Schubert was used to dealing with discouragement, and continued with the work he'd intended for Nägeli, the Piano Sonata in G major. It was completed in October and bought by the publisher Tobias Haslinger who brought it out in April 1827 under the title 'Fantasy'. It was a success with the music public and with the critics, though a review in the *Leipzig Musical News* contained an unwelcome comparison with Beethoven:

> *The composer, who has made for himself a numerous following by not a few excellent songs, is capable of doing the same by means of pianoforte pieces. He has evidently chosen Beethoven as a model. If that has its advantages for an artist of spirit and accomplishment such as Herr Schubert . . . it also has its dangers. To begin where a great master left off is fraught with peril . . . Beethoven appears to us to be in a class by himself . . . so that in truth he should not be chosen as an absolute model, since anyone who desired to be successful in that master's own line could only be himself.*

It was left to later generations of commentators, among them Alfred Einstein, to understand that it is precisely its independence from Beethoven which distinguishes this sonata.

Encouraged by Nägeli's approach, Schubert wrote in August to two publishers in Leipzig, Heinrich Probst and Breitkopf and Härtel, telling them that he was 'very desirous of becoming as well known as possible in Germany' and asking if they would care to

acquire some of his compositions 'on reasonable terms'. Probst's reply was encouraging – up to a point:

> *I am very gladly prepared to contribute towards the dissemination of your artistic reputation . . . Only I must frankly confess that our public does not yet sufficiently understand the peculiar, ingenious but perhaps now and then somewhat curious procedures of your mind's creations. Selected songs, not too difficult piano compositions for two and four hands, agreeable and comprehensible, would seem suitable for the attainment of your purpose and my wishes.*

Schubert sent three of his works (we don't know which ones), pricing them at 80 florins each, but that was evidently too much for Probst who said he was too busy publishing the complete works of the pianist-composer Friedrich Kalkbrenner to deal with Schubert's compositions. Breitkopf and Härtel, who would eventually publish the complete edition of Schubert's works fifty-six years after his death,

Schwind's impression of a Schubertiad at Spaun's house, probably in 1827

treated him in his lifetime as a novice. They offered to publish one of Schubert's works on a trial basis if he would accept free copies in lieu of a fee. Schubert did not bother to reply.

After countless revisions Schubert finished his 'Great' C major Symphony in the autumn of 1826 and decided to dedicate it to the Philharmonic Society. The hope, of course, was that the Society would agree to perform the symphony. At first they offered Schubert 100 florins 'not as a fee, but as a token of the Society's sense of obligation to you'. By the end of the year they'd agreed to have the parts copied. Then in the following year the Society's orchestra played through the symphony at one of their weekly rehearsals, after which it was announced that 'because of its length and difficulty', the symphony had been laid aside. It remained in limbo until 1839 when Schumann brought about the first performance by the Leipzig Gewandhaus orchestra with Mendelssohn conducting. It was not until the later decades of the nineteenth century that the symphony entered the general orchestral repertoire.

Beset as he was by professional disappointments, Schubert found a measure of escape by socialising with his friends, though the circle was as usual disrupted by petty quarrels from time to time. Two young law students from Linz, Franz and Fritz Hartmann, had recently joined the group, and according to them there were parties almost every evening often extending to one, two or three in the morning at The Green Anchor or Bogner's coffee-house. Around February 1827 they started frequenting The Castle of Eisenstadt. There was a grand-scale Schubertiad at Spaun's on 15 December, which is thought to have been the subject of Schwind's drawing of 1868. More than thirty people were invited and Vogl sang almost thirty of Schubert's songs. 'When the music was over, there was a glorious feed and then dancing' with Schubert and a friend providing piano duet accompaniment. Two days later there was an all-day party, starting with breakfast at Spaun's, followed by a drive to Nussdorf, followed by lunch, followed by music and dancing and conjuring tricks. Then it was back home for an evening at The Anchor. On 30 December the usual evening at The Anchor developed into a snowball fight between Spaun and Franz von Hartmann on one side and Schober, Schwind and Fritz von Hartmann on the other; Schubert kept out of it. A party at Schober's to see in the New Year – 1827 – was followed by a series of Schubertiads. One at Spaun's on 12 January for twenty guests boasted a four-hand piano sonata and several songs including 'Nacht und Träume', 'Im Abendrot' and the ever-popular 'Erlkönig'. When the party at Spaun's was over, every-one piled out to Bogner's with Schwind impersonating a vampire and pretending to fly. In February there were three musical evenings at Schober's, as Schober made the most of his last few weeks at his mother's roomy house. In March he and Schubert moved into a second-floor apartment in a house called 'The Blue Hedgehog'.

All these jollifications seem quite irrelevant to what was happening in Schubert's creative life. In an 1823 almanac he had come across twelve poems by the poet of *Die Schöne Müllerin*, Wilhelm Müller. 'Die Winterreise' inspired Schubert to create his greatest song-cycle, which he called simply *Winterreisse (Winter Journey)*. The sequence tells the story of a young man disappointed in love and disillusioned with life who struggles through snow and ice, reminded at every step of his isolation and despair. He eventually finds bleak comfort in identifying with the fate of the pathetic hurdy-gurdy man. Schubert imitates the monotonous drone characteristic of that instrument in his accompaniment to the final song of the cycle, 'Der Leiermann':

> *There beyond the village stands a hurdy-gurdy man,*
> *Grinding away with numb fingers as best he can.*
> *He stumbles barefoot to and fro on the ice*
> *And his little plate is always empty.*
> *No one wants to hear him,*
> *No one looks at him,*
> *And the dogs snarl round the old man.*
> *He takes it all as it comes;*
> *He goes on turning [the wheel which operates the instrument]*
> *And the hurdy-gurdy is never still.*
> *Strange old man, shall I go with you?*
> *Will you grind your hurdy-gurdy to my songs?*

Schubert's friends, as we have said, were well aware that there were two sides to his personality. Bauernfeld described his character as 'a mixture of tenderness and coarseness, sensuality and candour, sociability and melancholy'. Under the powerful influence of Müller's poems (Schubert set twelve of them in February and March, another twelve in October, making a sequence of twenty-four songs in all), the composer's underlying pessimism came to the surface yet again. His friends noticed a change in him, not least when he invited them all to his rooms on 4 March and failed to turn up himself. When Spaun asked him what was the matter, he replied: 'You will soon hear and understand'. The group did learn what had been going on when they accepted another invitation from Schubert soon afterwards: 'I will sing through a cycle of dreadful songs for you,' he promised them. 'I am curious to see what you think of them. I have been more affected by them than has been the case with other songs.

Beethoven's funeral in 1827. Schubert was among the escorts to the bier

These songs please me more than all of them.' They did not please the assembled company. Schober hated every one of the songs except 'Der Lindenbaum' with its nostalgic glimpse of happiness. But Schubert did not care. He knew the true measure of the *Winterreise* songs and told his friends: 'In time you will come to like them too.'

While Schubert was writing the first part of *Winterreise*, Vienna was coming to grips with the news that Beethoven was gravely ill. As his illness worsened and it became apparent that he was dying, the news spread beyond Vienna to the whole of Europe. From the Philharmonic Society of London, Beethoven received a gift of £100 to help with his expenses, while the publisher Schott sent him a dozen bottles of wine to ease his suffering. Others, fearing the worst, came to Vienna to pay their last respects. It's said that on or around 19 March Schubert visited Beethoven, together with Anton Schindler and Anselm and Josef Hüttenbrenner, but it's not certain the visit took place.

During a violent thunderstorm on 26 March, Beethoven died at the age of fifty-six. The funeral three days later was considered an event of such significance that Vienna's schools were closed. There was a long service, and the funeral procession was followed by a crowd of some 15–20,000 mourners. The bier was escorted by thirty-six Viennese musicians acting as torch-bearers with Schubert among them. 'All were clad in black,' said a newspaper report, 'with gloves of the same colour and streaming crêpe on the left arm, except the torch-bearers who for compensation had bunches of white lilies pinned on, whereas the torches were crêped.' In the evening Schubert joined Schober and Schwind among others at The Castle of Eisenstadt where they 'talked of nothing but Beethoven, his works and the well-merited honours paid to his memory'.

Beethoven's friend Anton Schindler said that he had shown some of Schubert's songs to Beethoven on his death-bed and the great man had remarked 'truly there is a divine spark in this Schubert.' Thus convinced of Beethoven's high opinion, Schindler passed on to Schubert some poems by Rellstab which Beethoven had not had time to set. This seemed to confirm a widespread expectation that Schubert would prove to be Beethoven's successor – an alarming burden for him to bear. Certainly many of his works in 1827 and 1828 reveal his respect for the deceased master.

During 1827 publishers vied with each other in bringing out compositions by Schubert, ranging from crowd-pleasing dance music, rondos and sets of variations to great songs. Even Diabelli saw the sense of swallowing his pride and repairing the relationship with Schubert which had been broken off in 1823: on 2 March he announced publication of four songs from *Wilhelm Meister* and two other songs, 'Drang in die Ferne' ('Distant Longing') and 'Auf dem Wasser zu singen' ('To be Sung on the Water').

Critical response was largely favourable. Berlin's *Musical News* highly recommended Schubert's songs in March and went on to express the hope 'that we shall ere long receive similar things by this excellent author'. When Schubert's Octet for Wind and Strings was performed at a concert in April, Vienna's *Theatre News* declared, 'Herr Schubert's composition is commensurate with the author's acknowledged talent: luminous, agreeable and interesting.' At a May concert, Schubert's 'Der Einsame' was the last minute substitute for a song by another composer and a reviewer asked, 'Who could fail to have been deeply touched, elevated and delighted by the profound and beautiful content of this song?' An element of official recognition came in June, when the Philharmonic Society promoted Schubert from deputy to full member of the Council of Representatives.

Robert Schumann

During June Schubert started work on Bauernfeld's forbidden opera *The Count of Gleichen* but set that aside to begin another project, his first set of four Impromptus. The title 'Impromptu' for a short piano composition was introduced by the Czech composer Wenzel Johann Tomaschek, and Schubert realised that it suited his poetic style and temperament after meeting one of Tomaschek's pupils at a Viennese party. Schubert composed a second set of four Impromptus in December 1827. In a similar category to the Impromptu is the 'Moment Musical': Schubert wrote four short pieces under this title in the summer of 1827.

The discovery of the second set of Müller's *Winterreise* poems at that time meant a temporary end to piano pieces, but during the autumn and winter, Schubert did find relief from the gloom of his *Winter Journey* in two major chamber works, the piano trios in B Flat and E Flat (though there's some doubt about the date of the composition of the first of them). Robert Schumann was among the influential admirers of these beautiful works, drawing a distinction between them by describing the B Flat trio as 'passive lyrical and feminine', and the E Flat trio by contrast as 'more spirited, masculine and dramatic'. One glance at the B Flat trio, said Schumann, 'and the troubles of our human existence disappear and all the world is bright and fresh again'. Hard to believe that it came from the pen of the man who wrote *Winterreise*.

On 2 September Schubert began a late-summer journey to Graz, headquarters of the Styrian Musical Society. His companion was Johann Jenger, a former resident of Graz who prompted the Society to organise a grand charity performance of Schubert works. The composer's hosts in Graz were friends of Jenger's, Carl and Marie Pachler, a couple very much at the centre of the town's musical scene.

Night after night their house resounded with songs, duets and waltzes by a man they were proud and delighted to welcome to their home.

Schubert and Jenger left for Vienna on 20 September. In his letter of thanks Schubert told Frau Pachler that he'd enjoyed 'the happiest days I have had for a long time. In Graz I soon discovered the natural and sincere way of keeping company.' Vienna, on the contrary, said Schubert, 'is devoid of cordiality, openness, genuine thought, meaningful words and especially sensible behaviour. There is so much confused chatter that one hardly knows whether one is being clever or stupid, and inward calm is seldom or never achieved.'

Marie Pachler had suggested Schubert should return to the poems of Gottfried von Leitner, and he did so in the autumn and winter, producing among other fine songs, 'Der Winterabend' and 'Die Sterne'. The stay in Graz itself had prompted rather lighter efforts, the twelve 'Graz Waltzes' and the 'Graz Galopp', followed in October by a little March in G for piano duet, which Schubert dispatched for Marie and her young son to play on Carl Pachler's name-day. In the accompanying letter Schubert sent his best wishes to Karl and added the ominous postscript: 'I hope your Grace is in better health than I, for my usual headaches are already plaguing me again.'

. VII .

A Last Chance

In spite of his headaches, or perhaps in a determined attempt to forget them, Schubert went on composing and socialising as vigorously as ever.

At the turn of the year, there was the usual New Year's Eve party at Schober's, and we know from the diary of one of the guests, Franz Hartmann, that it was a lively affair. 'On the stroke of twelve,' he wrote, 'we drank to a happy New Year in Malaga. Bauernfeld then read a poem. At two o'clock we made our way home, stopping in St Stephen's Square to congratulate Enk on his birthday . . . to Bogner's coffee-house.'

One verse of Bauernfeld's poem about the changes the New Year might bring, went as follows:

> The spells of the poet, the pleasures of singing,
> They too will be gone, be they true as they may;
> No longer will songs in our party be ringing,
> For the singer too will be called away.
> The waters from source to the sea must throng,
> The singer at last will be lost in song.

Bauernfeld can have had no idea how poignantly prophetic his words were, for there was nothing in Schubert's condition at the time to suggest that the Schubertians would lose their leader before 1828 was over. But he did know that the group was likely to split up, with each of the friends going his own way, and that this was likely to be the last New Year's Eve they would spend together.

They made the most of it. There was a relentless round of parties to start off the carnival season; with many of the core members of the group in town at least for a time, that old Schubertian pastime the Reading Party was revived. Almost every Saturday night between January and August 1828, the friends met at Schober's to share the pleasures of contemporary German literature – the writings of Heinrich von Kleist, Tieck, Goethe and others, not forgetting Schober's one and only published book of verse.

A sure sign of changing times was the announcement on 15 January of Josef von Spaun's engagement to Franziska Roner, described by Franz von Hartmann as 'thirty years of age, but very nice, cultivated and pretty'. Spaun had been the founder of the Schubertians, and on 28 January he hosted what was to prove his last Schubertiad, in honour of his fiancée. Among the fifty or so guests were members of the Schuppanzigh quartet – Schuppanzigh and the cellist Linke with pianist Karl Maria von Bocklet; together they performed Schubert's B Flat Piano Trio. After the music there was drinking and dancing until almost the entire company, according to Hartmann, was drunk. Then they all went off to Bogner's until 2.30 a.m. On 14 April, Spaun and Franziska were married.

Favourite haunts of the Schubertians in February were The Partridge coffee-house and The Snail; Schubert was usually there, as often as not with something to celebrate, since the early months of 1828 brought a flurry of performances and publications of his works. In January the Philharmonic Society did him proud with performances of choral and solo songs: there's the story that on the 24th, when his choral piece 'Ständchen' was given, Schubert had to be fetched from a bar to listen to it, remarking afterwards, 'I never realised it was so beautiful.' On 14 January the publisher Haslinger brought out Part 1 of *Winterreise*. Critical reaction was mixed, but there was plenty of praise, not least from Leipzig's *Allgemeine Musikalische Zeitung* which seems to have been well aware of Schubert's importance. Adverse comment tempered this: '[Schubert] likes to labour at harmonies for the sake of being new and piquant.' 'He is inordinately addicted to giving too many notes to the piano part, either at once or in succession.' And the same journal criticised the 'Fantasy in C for Piano and Violin' after a performance on 20 January. 'The verdict that might fairly be pronounced on it', declared the correspondent, 'is that the favourite composer has in this case positively miscomposed.' A view in harmony with that was expressed in Vienna's *Sammler*, with its reminder that the attention-span of the city's music lovers was limited: 'The Fantasy occupied rather too much of the time a Viennese is prepared to devote to pleasures of the mind. The hall emptied gradually, and the writer confesses that he too is unable to say anything about the conclusion of this piece of music.'

Song performances continued in February, and in March came a rave review of *Winterreise* in the *Theaterzeitung* soon after a gratifying appreciation of Schubert's genius in Dresden's *Abendzeitung*, from its Vienna correspondent:

> *Musical composition tends towards littleness . . . An honourable*
> *exception is made by the inspired Schubert with his songs. They*
> *have cleared a path for themselves through the welter, and this*
> *characteristic composer's name already sounds honourably from all*
> *lips, just as his songs are sung wherever triplet frippery has not yet*
> *ousted all feeling for truth and beauty.*

Meanwhile, favourable notices in German newspapers had their effect on German music-publishers and on 9 February Schubert heard from two of the most important of them (on the same day).

To be solicited by Probst of Leipzig must have given Schubert particular satisfaction, for when he had written to Probst back in 1826, he had been brushed off with the excuse that the firm was too busy. Now Probst wrote to say that, after studying some of Schubert's recent songs:

> *[He had] noticed how ever more clearly and soulfully you give utterance to your imagination. I have further taken delight in several four-handed works . . . which convince me that it would be easy to disseminate your name throughout the rest of Germany and the North. Kindly therefore send me anything you have finished to your satisfaction — songs, vocal pieces or romances which, without sacrificing any of your individuality, are yet not difficult to grasp; and also to assign to me some pieces for four hands of a similar kind.*

Even more flattering, in that there was no demand to keep things simple, was the letter from Schott of Mainz. That firm, founded in 1770, had acquired great eminence through the connection it had formed with Beethoven in 1824, and their letter said they would have approached Schubert sooner had they not been busy with the last of Beethoven's works. The letter continued:

> *We now take the liberty to request of you some works for publication. Piano works or vocal pieces for one or several voices, with or without piano accompaniment, will always be welcomed by us . . . You should know that we also have an establishment in Paris, where we shall likewise make your compositions known. If you have a number of things in stock and would like to send us a list of them, this would also be most agreeable to us.*

Given Probst's earlier treatment of him, it's not surprising that Schubert wrote first to Schott. On 21 February he offered the E Flat Piano Trio, the string quartets in D minor and G major, the second set of Impromptus, the Fantasy in F minor for piano duet and the one in C for piano and violin together with various solo songs and choruses and a comic trio. A week later Schott replied requesting all the works Schubert had proposed with the exception of the solo songs and string quartets. 'We should at once come to terms with you for all your works,' the letter explained, 'were it not that we are also obliged to carry out obligations entered into earlier; your works are all so attractive to a publisher that the choice is difficult.' Schott promised to publish the works he wanted 'by degrees and as soon as possible, and then to ask you anew for later works. You will please fix the lowest fee possible . . . Kindly advise us also of how many copies you wish to have for distribution to your friends.'

All this was very encouraging, and with visions of international fame in his mind, Schubert was confident enough to embark on his first (and, as it turned out, his last) organised concert. Ever since Beethoven's public concert of 7 May 1824, the Schubertians had been keen to stage a similar concert of Schubert's works, but they feared the consequences of failure, not least the effect on Schubert's reputation. The composer himself was more fearful than his friends, reminding them that Beethoven's concert had made a loss: that being the case, what chance had *he* got of succeeding?

It was Schubert's old friend Johann Jenger who convinced him otherwise. Jenger had for many years organised events for the Graz musical society, and he knew what to do to minimise risks and maximise profits. He persuaded the Philharmonic Society to let Schubert have their hall at The Red Hedgehog free of charge. Then he persuaded several leading musical performers, some of whom owed him for favours in the past, to take part in the concert. At the top of the bill was Schubert's long-time friend and admirer, the singer Michael Vogl; other attractions were the horn player Josef Lewy, the Schuppanzigh Quartet (minus Schuppanzigh who was ill), Josefine Fröhlich and her choir of young ladies from the Conservatoire, and the male-voice choir of the Philharmonic Society. With such an array of talent at his disposal, Schubert was able to arrange the kind of varied programme he knew would appeal to the Viennese.

A flowery announcement of the concert appeared in the *Theaterzeitung* on 25 March:

An invitation to Schubert's
only full-scale concert

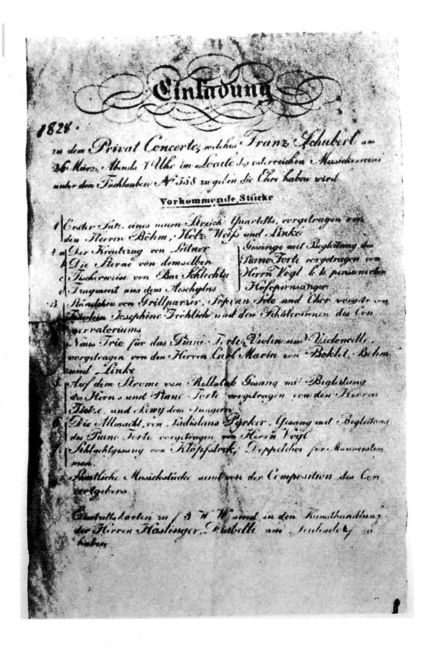

Franz Schubert, whose powerfully intellectual, enchantingly lovely
and original tone-poems have made him the favourite of the whole
musical public, and which may well secure their creator an
imperishable name by their genuine artistic value, will perform on 26
March a series of the latest products of his mind . . . May the glorious
German tone-poet, then, be granted an attendance such as his modesty

and unobtrusiveness would alone deserve, quite apart from his artistic eminence and that rare and great musical enjoyment which is to be expected.

There was a great demand for the 'tickets at three florins to be had at the art establishments of Diabelli, Haslinger and Leidesdorf', and on the 26 March (a date chosen by Schubert to coincide with the first anniversary of Beethoven's death) a crowd of more than 500 people crammed into the hall at The Red Hedgehog for a seven o'clock start.

The programme they were offered included only one piece specially composed for the concert: a setting for tenor solo with horn obbligato and piano accompaniment of a poem by Ludwig Rellstab, 'Auf dem Strom' ('On the River'). The poem explores the thoughts of a man as he sails out to sea, leaving behind his love, his youth and his innocence, and dreading the loneliness ahead. It was probably one of the poems Rellstab had sent to Beethoven and which had later been passed on to Schubert by Anton Schindler; the connection was underlined by a clear reference to the 'Eroica' Symphony's funeral march in Schubert's setting of the words. So the concert could be seen as both a graceful tribute to Beethoven, and a claim to the succession.

The first movement of the G major String Quartet was followed by a group of songs sung by Vogl. Then came 'Ständchen' ('Serenade') for soprano solo and chorus given by Josefine Fröhlich and her ladies from the Conservatoire after which the E Flat Trio was given complete. 'Auf dem Strom' came next followed by 'Die Allmacht' with Vogl. The finale was 'Schlachtgesang' ('Battle Song') a double chorus for male voices featuring the gentlemen of the Philharmonic Society.

It was all a great success. 'Everybody was lost in a frenzy of admiration and rapture,' wrote one member of the audience. Bauernfeld's comment bracketed enthusiasm with profit: 'Enormous applause, good receipts'. Not only had Schubert made his presence felt in public, he had lined his pocket to the tune of 320 florins. 'I shall never

*Paganini: Schubert thought
he played like an angel*

forget how glorious it was,' enthused Franz von Hartmann in his diary: 'To The Snail where we jubilated until midnight.'

There was just one snag. No report of the concert appeared in the Viennese press, for Schubert was upstaged by one of the most magnetic musicians of the age: he had to play second fiddle to Niccolò Paganini. Paganini had arrived in Vienna on 16 March, and the strange, sinister appearance of the Italian virtuoso, his scandalous life-style and extraordinary talents made him a journalist's dream. Since he appeared to come from another planet, stories invented by the press, however weird and wonderful, made perfect sense to a gullible and superstitious public. Many were ready to believe that Paganini had sold his soul to the devil.

Paganini gave his first concert on 29 March, and such was its amazing success that he remained in Vienna to give thirteen more concerts over a period of four months. People were prepared to pay what were regarded as extortionate prices: ten florins for the dress circle, five for the stalls – the five-florin note was renamed the Paganinerl by Viennese cab-drivers. When Paganini finally left Vienna, he was richer by 30,000 florins.

Paganini was obviously much more than a dazzling circus turn. The discerning Johann Jenger wrote to a friend: 'What you, dear lady, will read about him in the papers – and he receives much praise – is all too little. One can only hear, admire and wonder at him. More I cannot say.'

Schubert treated Bauernfeld to the Paganini concert on 4 May and was overwhelmed by his Second Concerto: 'I heard an angel sing in the adagio,' he told a friend afterwards.

Even though Schubert had deliberately planned his concert to include substantial works as well as songs, the Viennese critics, when they noticed him at all, persisted in referring to him as a 'well-known composer of Lieder and Romanzen'. Schubert had become accustomed to fairer assessments in the German press, and their Viennese correspondents did manage to refer to his concert. 'All these gentry and every piece they performed,' reported the Dresden *Abendzeitung*, 'were applauded more or less. There was unquestionably much that was good about it all, but the minor stars paled before the radiance of this comet [Paganini] in the musical heavens.' And it was only after a lengthy article on Paganini that Berlin's *Allgemeine Musikalische Zeitung* announced that at Schubert's concert 'the numerous gathering of friends and patrons did not stint [in] resounding applause after each number and saw to it that several were repeated'.

If press coverage of his concert was somewhat sparse, Schubert himself was not slow to report its success to the publishers who were showing interest in his work. Telling Probst he had not so far responded to his letter owing to the arrangements for the concert, he continued:

> It may perhaps not be without interest to you if I inform you that not only was the concert . . . crammed full, but also that I received extraordinary approbation. A Trio for piano, violin and cello in particular found general approval, so much so indeed that I have been invited to give a second concert. For the rest I can assign to you some works with pleasure if you will agree to the reasonable fee of 60 florins per sizeable book.

In reply to Schott's second letter, Schubert sent him the E Flat Trio, the second set of Impromptus and a male chorus ('Mondenschein') – rather less than he'd originally offered. And even this collection was too much for Schott, who wrote back accepting only the Impromptus and the chorus for a fee of 60 florins. 'The Trio is probably long,' the letter said, 'and as we have recently published several trios, we shall be obliged to defer that kind of composition until a little later, which might not after all be to your advantage.'

In fact the Trio was accepted for publication by Probst, who took Schubert's letter to mean that he could have it for 60 florins. Schubert dispatched it grudgingly: 'Herewith I am sending you the desired Trio, although a song or piano book was understood for the price of 60 florins, and not a Trio for which six times as much work is required. In order, however, to make a beginning at last, I would ask only for the speediest possible publication, and for the dispatch of six copies.' Probst responded with a request for a title, dedication and opus number. 'The opus number of the Trio is 100,' Schubert replied. 'The work is to be dedicated to nobody, save those who find pleasure in it. That is the most profitable dedication.'

Yet another German publisher, Karl Brüggemann, also showed interest, but once again the accent was on simplicity. He asked Schubert to contribute piano pieces to a collection to be published in monthly instalments called *Mühling's Museum*, specifying that 'the original compositions to be included must not be too difficult but may on the contrary be quite easy . . . they should not be more than two pages long'. Schubert must have responded positively, because a second letter from Brüggemann expressed his continued eagerness: 'I am very glad that you, sir, are inclined to furnish compositions for *Mühling's Museum* and I await your kind consignments.' Whether Brüggemann ever received any consignments is not known.

Meanwhile, Haslinger continued to publish songs, and brought out the attractive 'Moments Musicaux'. *Winterreise* attracted a rave review in Vienna's *Zeitschrift für Kunst* which ended: 'We congratulate the gifted composer with all our hearts on so well-made and beautiful a work and gladly await its sequel.' A comment which has to be set against the verdict of Berlin's *Allgemeine Musikalische Zeitung* to the effect that Müller's sequence of verses was far too long: 'It might have made one good song had it not become twenty-four of them.' Performances of Schubert's music also continued through the late spring and early summer of 1828. The audience called for an encore when the setting of Psalm 23 for women's chorus was given in May, a month which also brought the first performance at Bauernfeld's of one of Schubert's greatest work for piano duet, the Fantasy in F minor composed earlier in the year.

Although Schubert had benefited financially from his concert, he longed for a more stable source of income, setting his sights on a musical post in the church. Perhaps he entertained ideas of succeeding the

Schubert enjoys a sundowner with Lachner and Bauernfeld

63-year-old Imperial Kapellmeister Josef Eybler — as it turned out, Eybler survived Schubert by nearly twenty years. During the summer of 1828 Schubert began to enlarge his portfolio of sacred works, seeking by and large to please the Viennese taste for sentimentality in church music. He produced a 'Hymn to the Holy Ghost' for male quartet and chorus, 'Faith, Hope and Love' for vocal quartet, chorus and windband, and a setting in Hebrew of Psalm 92 for Salomon Sulzer, Cantor of the new Vienna Synagogue, which was enjoying a revival since the easing in 1826 of official restrictions on the Jewish community.

Schubert's renewed interest in writing for the church resulted in one masterpiece, the Mass No. 6 in E Flat, composed in June. This demonstrated Schubert's mastery of the contrapuntal skills traditionally required of a church composer, which had never been among Schubert's strong suits. On this occasion, in order to remedy a weakness he was well aware of, he set about studying the fugues of Mozart, in particular the Fugue in G minor which served as a model for Schubert's Fugue in E minor for organ. He composed this on 3 June after a discussion on counterpoint with his composer friend Franz Lachner while they were both staying at an inn in Baden. Lachner challenged Schubert to a fugue-writing competition and the pair of them went to the Heiligenkreuz monastery north-west of Baden to try out the results. We don't know who won.

In June and July Schubert spent some weeks with Schober at the Schobers' summer residence in Währing. By then the proceeds of the concert had run out, part of the money no doubt spent on drugs and consultations with his doctor, Ernst Rinna, for Schubert was still suffering from terrible headaches.

His way of life did nothing to improve his health. Working feverishly, he didn't bother about proper meals, even if he could have afforded them. According to Bauernfeld he 'lived on apples and fritters for supper . . . so that no one can see into the inside of his soul and empty purse'. On one occasion Bauernfeld found Schubert wolfing down six croissants with coffee having eaten nothing else all day. But if Schubert cut down on food to save a few pennies, the drinking went on apace. A party on 29 June ended with everyone drunk, 'Schubert especially'.

Shortage of cash interfered with his holiday plans that summer. There had been a proposal to spend a holiday with Jenger at the Pachlers' house in Graz, but this had to be postponed twice, the second time owing to 'the not very brilliant financial circumstances of friend Schubert'. As Jenger explained in a letter of 4 July to Frau Pachler, these 'circumstances' were spoiling other projects too:

*Schubert had planned to spend part of the summer at Gmunden
[but] . . . has so far been prevented by the above-mentioned financial
embarrassments. He is still here at present, works diligently at a new
mass and only awaits still — wherever it may come from — the
necessary money to take his flight into Upper Austria. In these
circumstances, our excursion to Graz may thus take its turn at the
beginning of September.*

It never did.

Incessant work distracted Schubert from thoughts of holidays.
Having completed three settings of poems by Ludwig Rellstab earlier
in the year (including 'Auf dem Strom', performed with success at his
concert), Schubert composed in August seven further Rellstab settings, among them 'Ständchen' ('Serenade'). Having come across the
work of Heinrich Heine at the reading parties in January, Schubert
created settings of six Heine poems, all of them masterpieces, including 'Der Atlas' ('Atlas') and 'Der Doppelgänger' ('The Ghostly
Double'), together with a love-song (composed later in October) to
words by one of Schubert's favourite local poets, Johann Seidl, 'Die
Taubenpost' ('Pigeon Post').

This 1828 group of songs embraces an enormous range of moods,
subjects and styles, and in no way did Schubert think of them as swan
songs. It was the publisher Tobias Haslinger who, in April 1829, five
months after Schubert's death, brought out the songs by Rellstab,
Heine and Seidl as a single collection under the title *Schwanengesang*,
hoping no doubt that the composer's grieving admirers would want to
acquire an anthology of his recent utterances.

During September, Schubert completed four masterpieces — the
String Quintet in C major, with its heartbreaking slow movement,
and three piano sonatas. These are large-scale works in which
Schubert truly found his independent voice as a keyboard composer.
The C-minor is the most reminiscent of Beethoven — heroic, stormy,
dramatic, dark and mysterious. The A-major is more varied in mood,
at times serious and menacing, at others exuberant and lighthearted:

it refers to two of Schubert's songs, 'Pilgerweise' and 'Im Frühling'. The B-flat major, after its ominous opening, is serene and contemplative and the most poetic of the three. The story goes that Schubert finished his sonatas just in time to perform them at a party given by Dr Ignaz Menz on 27 September.

Extreme pressure of work, too little food and probably too much drink resulted in further deterioration in Schubert's health and, on the advice of Dr Rinna, he had moved at the beginning of September from the centre of the city to the new suburb of Wieden. There he stayed with his brother, hoping that the fresher air on the city's outskirts would do him good, though he continued to pay the rent at his lodgings, thinking that he would be able to return there in due course. Dr Rinna must have thought that with his brother feeding and looking after him, Schubert would regain his strength. But while Ferdinand and his family ministered to his brother's every physical need, they could not persuade him to slow down and rest. His mind was full of music, and it had to be brought to birth.

At the beginning of September Schubert was hopeful that his publishers would come up with the money he needed for a holiday, but on the 25th he had to write to Jenger: 'Nothing will come of the trip to Graz this year, for money and weather are wholly unfavourable.' On 2 October he wrote to both Schott and Probst, desperate for news of his compositions. He asked Probst when the E Flat trio would appear, and offered the three piano sonatas, the Heine songs and the Quintet in C. From Schott he wanted to know the fate of his Impromptus and the five-part chorus he had sent him.

Probst had the courtesy to reply quickly, apologising for the delay in bringing out the Trio and asking to see the Heine songs; Schott's reply was depressing and insulting. The letter explained that they'd had a negative response from their Paris branch, which had returned the Impromptus 'with the intimation that these works are too difficult for trifles and would find no outlet in France'. As for the five-part chorus, the letter promised publication soon, but continued: 'We are bound to observe that this small opus is too dear at the fee fixed, for the whole occupies but six printed pages in the piano part, and we assume that it is by some error that we are asked to pay 60 florins for this. We offer you 30 florins.' That was the end of Schubert's dealings with Schott.

Early in October, Schubert did manage a short holiday, a pilgrimage on foot to Haydn's grave in Eisenstadt, Hungary. His companions were his brother Ferdinand and two choirmaster friends of his, Josef Mayssen and Johann Rieder. Such company prompted Schubert to think of church music again and on his return to Vienna he wrote another two liturgical settings, 'Intende Voci' and 'Tantum Ergo', as well as his last two songs, 'Die Taubenpost' and 'Der Hirt auf dem Felsen' ('The Shepherd on the Rock'). This beautiful extended aria for soprano, clarinet and piano was composed for Anna Milder-Hauptmann, prima donna of the Berlin opera. It was performed for the first time in March 1830 and then left in oblivion until 1902.

On the last day of October, Schubert went out with Ferdinand and friends for dinner at The Red Cross. He took one mouthful of the fish he'd ordered, then bolted from the restaurant, complaining that his food tasted like poison. But although he couldn't eat, he continued with his busy life. On 3 November he attended a performance of Ferdinand's Requiem Mass, then went on a three-hour walk. Next day, still worried about his inadequate contrapuntal technique, he began lessons in fugue and counterpoint with court organist Simon Sechter, the man who would one day instruct Liszt and Bruckner.

Before he could start on the homework Sechter had given him (to write a fugue on the musical equivalent of his own name) Schubert fell ill again. He hadn't eaten anything for days and assumed that that was the cause of his condition, telling Spaun: 'There is nothing really the matter with me, except that I am so exhausted I feel as if I were going to fall through the bed.' He got no better and on 12 November wrote to another of his closest friends: 'Dear Schober, I am ill. I have eaten nothing for eleven days, and drunk nothing, and I totter feebly and shakily from my chair to bed and back again. Rinna is treating me. If I take anything, I bring it up at once.'

Schubert's symptoms, unpleasant though they were, seemed to be confined to his digestive system. He wasn't feverish, he talked of weakness rather than pain, and his mind was as active as ever. He did as his doctors told him, even keeping a watch beside his bed so as not to miss the prescribed doses, but was unable to rest mentally. He implored Schober to send him some novels to relieve the boredom and demanded from visiting friends news of what was happening in Vienna. When they reported that Beethoven's quartet in C sharp minor Op. 131 had just been published, Schubert expressed his longing to hear it. So his friends arranged a bedside performance which caused Schubert the utmost delight: but the emotion he felt was so powerful that it left him weaker than ever.

On the morning of 17 November, Schubert was visited by Bauernfeld and Lachner and was well enough to discuss with them the ill-fated opera *Der Graf von Gleichen*. When they left he was in good spirits, but later that day his health deteriorated so dramatically that Ferdinand called in a male nurse to help his wife Anna and Schubert's step-sister Josefa care for him. By the next day Schubert was delirious and had to be forcibly restrained from getting out of bed; the day after, 19 November, at three o'clock in the afternoon, he died, two months short of his thirty-second birthday. The sequence of events that day was recalled thus by brother Ferdinand: 'All day long he wanted to get up, and continued to imagine that he was in a strange room. A few hours later the doctor appeared . . . But Schubert looked fixedly into the doctor's eyes, grasped at the wall with a feeble hand, and said, slowly and seriously: "Here, here is my end."'

So what was the cause of death? In *Music and Medicine*, John O'Shea states, 'Typhoid fever, then an extremely common illness, best fits the known facts,' even though fever was not present until towards the end. Wieden, where Ferdinand lived, was a new suburb and the sewage arrangements were incomplete, so the surroundings may have been less salubrious than central Vienna. But given Schubert's general state of health, a less virulent infection might have been enough to

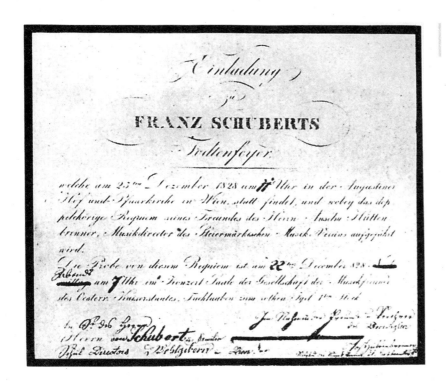

finish him off. Can it be coincidence that when Dr Rinna fell ill during his treatment of Schubert, he handed him over to a specialist in venereal diseases, Dr Josef von Vering? Vering's diagnosis, conveyed to us via his nephew, was that, owing to 'advanced decomposition of the blood', Schubert would never recover. He didn't say what had caused his blood to 'decompose'. Perhaps it was the mercury treatment he had undergone for syphilis.

Schubert's funeral took place at St Joseph's church in the Margareten suburb on Friday 21 November, a private service for friends and family. Schober, who for whatever reason had not visited Schubert during his illness, wrote some special words for the composer's 'Pax Vobiscum'. Schubert would have been buried at St Joseph's too, if the family had not decided on another plan.

On the morning of the funeral Ferdinand wrote to their father to propose that, if at all possible, they should lay Franz to rest at the Währing cemetery. He was acting on a conversation he'd had with his delirious brother the night before he died:

> Franz: *'I implore you to transfer me to my room, not to leave me in*
> *this corner under the earth; do I then deserve no place above the*
> *earth?'*
> Ferdinand: *'Dear Franz, rest assured, believe your brother Ferdinand*
> *whom you have always trusted and who loves you so much. You are*
> *in the room where you have always been and lie in your own bed.'*
> Franz: *'No it is not true. Beethoven does not lie here!'*

Ferdinand understood from this that Schubert wanted nothing more than to 'repose by the side of Beethoven, whom he so greatly revered'. His father agreed to find the 70 florins required to transfer the body of his son to Währing and Schubert was duly buried three graves along from Beethoven.

The cost of the funeral was not covered by what Schubert left behind. There was no money. There was no will. Some clothes, some bedding, a mattress and some old music (not his own) raised 63 florins. But in the months to come, Ferdinand did recoup the funeral expenses by selling Schubert's manuscripts, most of which reposed in a cabinet at Schober's house.

The world took some time to realise what it had lost. Eventually in 1863, Schubert's remains were exhumed along with those of Beethoven. 'The advanced state of decay of the skeleton,' writes John O'Shea, 'was held to be due to the presence of syphilitic disease of the bone, or possibly to mercurial damage caused by medication.' In 1888, the two bodies, or what remained of them, found their final resting-place in the Musicians' Grove of Vienna's new Central cemetery. Schubert and Beethoven lie next to a monument to Mozart.

The grief of Schubert's friends in the immediate aftermath of his death is conveyed in touching letters and diary entries. On the day after Schubert's death, Bauernfeld wrote: 'Yesterday afternoon Schubert died. On Monday I still spoke with him. On Tuesday, he was delirious, on Wednesday dead. To the last he talked to me of our opera. It all seems like a dream to me. The most honest soul and the

*Schubert's grave, near to
Beethoven and Mozart in
Vienna's central cemetery*

most faithful friend! I wish I lay there in his place.' After the funeral he wrote, with a touch of self-pity: 'Buried our Schubert yesterday. Schober with his art establishment is near bankruptcy Schwind and I are discouraged. What a life this is!'

Schwind, who had always shown intense devotion to Schubert, heard the news in Munich where he was now living. He wrote to 'dear good Schober':

You know how much I cared for him, and you may imagine that I could hardly grasp the thought of having lost him. We still have friends, dear and well-meaning ones, but there is none left who has lived that precious and memorable time with us and has not forgotten it. I have wept for him as a brother, but I am now glad for him that he died in his greatness and has done with his sorrows. The more I realise now what he was like, the more I see what he has suffered.

On Christmas Eve, he expressed in another letter to Schober what all the Schubertians were thinking: 'Schubert is dead and with him all that we had of the brightest and fairest.'

There was a memorial service on 23 December at the church of St Augustine, with a performance of Anselm Hüttenbrenner's Requiem for double choir. Afterwards there was a gathering at Spaun's. At about that time Grillparzer and the Fröhlichs launched a campaign to collect funds for a memorial, and in January 1829 there was a private concert in the Philharmonic Society hall which raised half the money. Schober was asked to design the monument, which was eventually erected in 1830. Grillparzer was asked to think of a suitable inscription, and the friends chose: 'The art of music here entombed a rich possession, but even fairer hopes.'

Postlude

The world's assessment of Schubert in 1828 was very different from the way we think of him in 1997. Even his most sympathetic admirers had no notion of the true scale of his achievement. 'For all the admiration I have given the dear departed for years,' said Spaun to Bauernfeld in 1839, 'I still feel that we shall never make a Mozart or a Haydn of him in instrumental or church compositions, whereas in song he is unsurpassed.'

Spaun's qualified view of Schubert's greatness is understandable, for less than half of Schubert's huge output had been published in his lifetime, and for the most part the works that *had* appeared were the less weighty ones. Still hidden from view were nine symphonies, ten operas, eighteen string quartets, two quintets, eighteen piano sonatas, six masses, about eighty pieces for vocal groups and six hundred songs.

Ferdinand found a ready market for the songs when, in November 1829, he offered Diabelli a huge pile of manuscripts including 'all the songs for solo voice with piano accompaniment'. Diabelli bought the lot for 2,400 florins. Between 1830 and 1851 he brought out the songs in fifty instalments, but left a stack of chamber and piano music to gather dust on his shelves. In fact Diabelli hadn't acquired quite all the songs. In December 1829, Ferdinand sold the thirteen songs which were to make up *Schwanengesang* plus 'The Shepherd on the Rock' to Haslinger for 290 florins: Haslinger also bought the last three piano sonatas for 70 florins each.

The works which had come off the presses did little at this stage to alter the world's view of Schubert's status. In 1828 the British musicologist Edward Holmes wrote an article on musical life in Vienna without a single reference to Schubert, and in 1834 when the music historian Raphael Georg Kieswetter finished a chapter called 'The Epoch of Beethoven and Rossini' in his *History of European-Occidental Music*, again it contained no mention of Schubert, despite the fact that Kieswetter had known the composer. A century had to pass before Schubert achieved the kind of fame and reputation which had come to Rossini and Beethoven in their lifetime.

In 1835 Ferdinand made a very good move. He decided to advertise his brother's remaining manuscripts in the pages of an influential musical periodical: the *Neue Zeitschrift für Musik*, whose editor at that time was Robert Schumann. The magazine had a wide circulation in Germany and Austria, but there were no takers. However, the advertisement had aroused Schumann's interest, and when he went to Vienna in the autumn of 1838 he knocked on Ferdinand's door. The two men met a few times to talk about Schubert and his music, and on New Year's Day the following year, Ferdinand decided to reveal his store of manuscripts. 'Finally Ferdinand allowed me to see some of Franz Schubert's compositions,' wrote Schumann. 'The riches that lay here piled up made me tremble with pleasure. Where to begin, where to stop?'

When he came to the 'Great' C major Symphony, Schumann could hardly believe his eyes. 'Who knows how long it would have lain neglected there in dust and darkness,' Schumann wrote, 'if I had not immediately arranged for Ferdinand Schubert to send it to the management of the Gewandhaus concerts in Leipzig, to the artist himself who conducts them' (this was Felix Mendelssohn). How fortunate it was that the symphony was seen by someone capable of recognising a work of genius, and of securing a performance by one of Europe's leading orchestras within three months of its discovery.

On 21 March 1839 Mendelssohn conducted the Leipzig Gewandhaus orchestra in the première of the 'Great' C major. That was enough to secure the work a permanent place in the orchestra's repertoire, but Schumann was exaggerating when he claimed that the piece aroused 'almost universal admiration'. When in December 1839 the Vienna Philharmonic deigned to perform two movements of the 'Great' with an operatic aria sandwiched between them, a critic declared that 'Schubert seemed to be unable fully to succeed with the tonal masses. The result was a kind of skirmish of instruments out of which no effectual pattern emerged . . . in my opinion it would have been better to leave the work entirely alone.'

Which is what the conductor of an orchestra in Paris decided to do when his players proved unequal to the symphony's demands, and in London even Mendelssohn was obliged to give up his attempt to perform it when, in 1844, a handful of players in the orchestra of the Royal Philharmonic Society ridiculed parts of the last movements at rehearsal. However, the New World redressed the balance of the old when the New York Philharmonic gave a performance of the 'Great' in January 1851.

Meanwhile, another powerful champion had emerged on behalf of Schubert: Franz Liszt. Liszt spent his teenage years in Paris and there he encountered a Belgian musician by the name of Chrétien Urhan who was busily promoting Schubert's music, particularly his songs, which soon became an established feature in Parisian musical life. In 1843 Heinrich Heine would remark that Paris was inundated with songs by 'an unidentified Monsieur Schubert', in response to which Diabelli would later bring out an edition of Schubert's *lieder* with French as well as German words.

When Liszt went to Vienna in 1838 to give a series of concerts to raise funds for a Beethoven memorial, he not only accompanied Schubert's 'Die Forelle' to great acclaim but included his own piano

Mendelssohn, who conducted the first performance of the 'Great' C major Symphony

transcription of the 'Ave Maria'. This was a harbinger of things to come, for Liszt was eventually to produce transcriptions of some fifty Schubert songs, four of them for orchestra and the rest for piano. Diabelli and Haslinger competed in their eagerness to publish the transcriptions as soon as they appeared, and Haslinger badgered Liszt for more. 'Haslinger overwhelms me with Schubert,' Liszt complained, 'I have just sent him twenty-four more new songs . . . and for the moment I am rather tired of this work.' Liszt attracted adulation wherever he went, and his performances of the song transcriptions brought Schubert's name before a much wider public than it had reached hitherto. What's more the transcriptions were, in their own right, sensitive works of art. Liszt was very careful to preserve the poetry and drama of Schubert's originals; for example, in 'Erlkönig' he uses a different register on the keyboard to represent the three characters of the boy, the father and the Erlking. He always insisted that the words of the song should be printed above the stave, so that a pianist would not forget what the poem was about. Apart from the songs, Liszt was deeply impressed by Schubert's *Wanderer Fantasy*, with its pioneering use of the 'transformation of themes'. Liszt made an arrangement of the work for piano and orchestra, and Schubert's compositional method helped to shape his own symphonic poems.

In 1849 Schubert's chamber music began to be revealed to the world, thanks to the violinist Josef Hellmesberger and his quartet. Masterpieces like the Quartet in D minor, the C major Quintet and the Octet were brought before the public at a series of concerts in the 1850s and '60s. Present at many of them was the famous critic Eduard Hanslick who in 1862 expressed his amazement at what he was hearing. 'Schubert has been dead for over thirty years, yet it is as though he continued to work invisibly. One can hardly keep up with him.'

When Brahms arrived in Vienna in the same year, he came across yet another stack of unpublished Schubert scores:

My best hours here I owe to the unprinted works of Schubert, of which I have quite a number at home in manuscript. Yet however delightful and enjoyable it is to contemplate them, everything else about this music is sad. I have many things here belonging to [the publisher] Spina or to [Schubert's nephew] Schneider of which nothing exists but the manuscript, not a single copy. And neither at Spina's nor with me are they kept in fireproof cabinets.

Brahms did eventually persuade his own publisher, Rieter-Biedemann, to accept some of Schubert's manuscripts including the Mass in E flat.

In England Schubert's songs became drawing-room favourites, especially after Queen Victoria and Prince Albert developed a taste for them, encouraged no doubt by their friend Mendelssohn; but the 'Great' C major Symphony had a long battle for acceptance. August Manns, conductor of the Crystal Palace Saturday concerts, recalled that he was 'frequently urged to avoid the works of unknown and unappreciated composers, amongst whom at that time were Schubert and Schumann'. But knowing of Schumann's and Mendelssohn's opinion of the symphony, he acquired a copy of the score. In 1856, twelve years after the work's rejection by the Philharmonic Orchestra, Manns introduced it to a British audience for the first time. Manns failed to convince the secretary to the Saturday concerts, Mr George Grove, that the 'Great' should become a regular feature on Saturdays and after one further airing it stayed in the cupboard for ten years, resurfacing in April 1866.

By that time not only had George Grove overcome his initial reservations, but he had become an important new recruit to the Schubert cause. Stunned by the beauty of the *Rosamunde* overture when Manns introduced him to it, he became aware, from the first full-length biography of Schubert by the German scholar Kreissle von Hellborn published in 1865, of the existence of Schubert's earlier symphonies and of other items associated with *Rosamunde*. Grove sent an urgent request to Spina (Diabelli's successor) who responded by sending two entr'actes from *Rosamunde* which he'd recently published. These were given in London in November 1866, and, according to Grove, 'at once created an extraordinary impression among the critics present'. In response to a request for more, Spina sent to London two more extracts from the Rosamunde music, but three numbers were still missing.

Meanwhile, the 'Unfinished' Symphony had come to light in Graz in the house of Anselm Hüttenbrenner and Ludwig Herbeck had conducted the first performance in Vienna on 17 December 1865. It was published early in 1867 and on 6 April that year Manns conducted the British première at Crystal Palace. To the two existing movements he added the Entr'acte in B minor from *Rosamunde*, a practice which continued for over half a century. In the 1920s, to mark the centenary of Schubert's death, a prize was offered to the best completion of the 'Unfinished' Symphony. Happily today we are content with what Schubert alone composed.

That April performance decisively sharpened Grove's appetite for more. 'I eagerly asked everyone whom I met,' he remembered, 'Mr Joachim, Madam Schumann and others, for information as to the rest of the symphonies, but without success; no one had seen them or knew anything about them.' Grove was convinced they were languishing in some dark corner in Vienna and on 5 October he arrived in the city with fellow Schubert enthusiast Arthur Sullivan. The publisher Spina put them in touch with Schubert's nephew Dr Eduard Schneider, who'd inherited Schubert's unpublished manuscripts. 'A quarter of an hour's conversation was sufficient to put us perfectly en rapport,' reported Grove, 'and soon I had the scores of the first, second, third, fourth and sixth of Schubert's symphonies in my hands.' But what Grove wanted above all was a complete *Rosamunde* score. Spina had given him a little more material, but there were still ingredients missing, and the proper order of the items was unknown. It looked as though Grove and Sullivan would have to leave without what they most wanted.

Having almost given up, they paid a final farewell call on Dr Schneider. Once again, Grove turned the conversation to the *Rosamunde* music and Schneider said he believed he had had, at one time, a copy or sketch of it. 'Might I go into the cupboard and look for it?' asked Grove. 'Certainly, if you have no objection to being smothered with dust,' replied Schneider.

In I [Grove] went and after some search, during which my companion kept the Doctor engaged in conversation, I found at the bottom of the cupboard and in its farthest corner, a bundle of music books two feet high, carefully tied round, and black with the undisturbed dust of nearly half a century . . . I dragged out the bundle into the light and

> *found that it was actually neither more nor less that what we were in*
> *search of . . . the part-books of the whole of the* Rosamunde *music,*
> *tied up after the second performance in December 1823, and probably*
> *never disturbed since.*

Schneider allowed Grove and Sullivan to copy the *Rosamunde* parts they were lacking, a task so laborious that they enlisted the aid of a Viennese musical friend and worked till two in the morning, after which Grove and Sullivan let off steam in a game of leapfrog before retiring for the night. Not long after their return to London, Manns conducted the first ever complete performance of the *Rosamunde* music at the Crystal Palace.

Grove's account of the discovery of the early symphonies and the *Rosamunde* music appeared as an appendix to the 1869 English edition of Kreissle von Hellborn's Schubert biography. The final paragraph reflects the bitterness he felt about the world's neglect of the composer:

> *Certainly what poor Schubert said was right, that the music that*
> *was the fruit of his distress had given the world most pleasure; and*
> *the world must have known it, for it kept him in his poverty and*
> *harassment and disappointment till he died of it. Good God! It makes*
> *one's blood boil to think of so fine and rare a genius, one of the ten or*
> *twelve topmost men in the world, in want of even the common*
> *necessities of life.*

Grove wrote a lengthy piece on Schubert in his *Dictionary of Music and Musicians*, first published in 1879, and in 1881 Manns conducted all the symphonies one after another in chronological order. The same year the millionaire Nicholas Dumba bought many of the manuscripts that remained in Schneider's collection for 6,000 florins, and in 1884 Breitkopf and Härtel brought out the first volume in their complete edition of Schubert's works, a project which had taken them thirteen years.

So the world at last was beginning to learn the true extent of Schubert's achievements. But as Schubert's music became popular, critical voices arose to declare that Schubert was unworthy of all the adulatory fuss. Romain Rolland, Vincent D'Indy, Hubert Parry and Richard Wagner were among those who took that line, and Bernard Shaw, writing as a music critic under the *nom de plume* Corno di Bassetto, expressed disapproval of the annual repetitions of the 'Great' C major Symphony under Manns:

> *In the Crystal Palace there is an understanding among the regular*
> *frequenters that a performance of Schubert's Symphony in C is one of*
> *the specialities of the place. The analytic programme of it is one of Sir*
> *George Grove's masterpieces and Mr Manns always receives a special*
> *ovation at the end . . . I have to make a point of looking pleased, lest*
> *Sir George should turn my way and, reading my thoughts, cut me dead*
> *for ever afterwards. For it seems to me almost wicked to give the public*
> *so irresistible a description of all the manifold charms and*
> *winningness of this astonishing symphony and not tell him, on the*
> *other side of the question, that a more exasperatingly brainless*
> *composition was never put on paper.*

Even more damaging to a proper assessment of Schubert was the image of the man generated by some of his most devoted admirers. In his 1865 biography, Hellborn was too ready to accept anecdotal evidence about Schubert's character and presented the world with a picture of a jolly smiling little fellow who lived it up with his friends and his women in the cafés of Biedermeier Vienna. Drawing on such material the theatre and cinema in the early twentieth century conspired to project this cosy individual as the real Schubert. There was a one-act play by Johann Raudnitz called *Hark, Hark the Lark* depicting a love triangle between Schubert, Therese Grob and Karoline Esterházy, and in 1916 came the Heinrich Berté operetta *Das Dreimädlerhaus* which became *Lilac Time* in Britain and *Blossom Time* in America, and gave rise to a sickly film starring Richard Tauber.

It's only in the last fifty years that we have developed a more realistic view of Schubert, largely thanks to the labours of Professor Otto Erich Deutsch, who in 1946 published his compilation of all the hard-and-fast facts of Schubert's life, leaving the romantic legend without a leg to stand on. He did Schubert another great service in 1948 with his Thematic Catalogue – hence the 'D' numbers now used to identify the composer's works.

While the sugary image of Schubert the man persisted, performances of his music were also apt to be over-romanticised. Then came Arturo Toscanini, with his passion for playing everything as the composer wrote it. 'Toscanini wiped out the arbitrariness of the post-romantic interpreters,' wrote his fellow conductor Georg Szell. 'He did away with the meretricious tricks and the thick incrustation of interpretive nuances that had been building up for decades.'

In this respect Toscanini was the herald of the present age in which the quest for authenticity is one of the dominating aims of the musical world. That quest, applied across the vast range of Schubert's creative output, is perhaps helping us at last, two hundred years after his birth, to a truer understanding of one of the world's greatest and most beloved composers.

Index

Page numbers in *italics* denote illustrations.